Strokes

Strokes

essays and reviews 1966 - 1986

John Clute

Cosmos Books, an imprint of **Wildside Press**
New Jersey . New York . California . Ohio

Strokes

Published by:

Cosmos Books, an imprint of Wildside Press
P.O. Box 45, Gillette, NJ 07933-0045
www.wildsidepress.com

For more information, contact Wildside Press.

ISBN: 1-58715-384-X

Contents///

//An Introduction to Clute

Thomas M. Disch

I can say I knew him when, when being in this case a quarter-century ago in 1961. We were at N.Y.U.'s Washington Square College, taking the same two courses — *The Quest for Utopia* (4 points, taught by Professor Patrick of the English department) and *Western Intellectual History* (3 points, with the History department's Professor Falnes). Those two courses, those two teachers, and John represent the most palpable dent that my college years managed to make on my sense of myself as a pure autodidact, for whom schooling was no more than a rite of passage that had to be performed with ceremonious correctness while the essential process of education was carried on at home and at the library.

Clute was much the same sort of conceited know-it-all, yet here (in these two courses) were texts neither of us had read, nor even known we ought to. Here were bibliographies and vistas of history that made a mockery of our fledgling shelves of paperbacks, of our ability to discourse on the deeper meanings of Kafka and Joyce and the other Modern Masters who formed that era's canon of what an English major should have read. In fact (at last I dare confess it), Clute had actually read more of those books than I had, and *knew* more about the world they shadowed forth than I did, and this despite the disadvantages he suffered (as I then supposed) of being the son of the chief officer of a New York bank (entrusted at times with his father's limo).

He'd read the *hard* poets, like Crane and Stevens, whose oeuvres I only pretended to have read; he'd penetrated deep into the thickets of the most mandarin critics, like Empson and Frye, and, more, he'd assimilated their critical (and poetic) vocabularies and was able to use them himself to tie just the right bow on the term papers in which he practised his first acts of criticism.

These were peculiar attainments for an undergraduate in the early 60's at N.Y.U., where the most ambitious students were on a career track to medical, law, and business schools. But what was still more peculiar in John's appetite for *belles lettres* was his indifference to distinctions of highbrow and lowbrow. In those days literary academics were much more confidently disdainful of "mass culture" than has since come to be the case. A few credentialed intellectuals like Barzun and Auden would admit to having occasionally read and enjoyed a mystery or two, and there was a small pantheon of film directors who could be discussed by the truly Serious. But science fiction? That was entirely outside the pale of literary respectability.

Nevertheless, John read the stuff, and he read each novel and story with the same passion for squeezing out all its hermeneutical juices ("hermeneutical" is a word I picked up from John) that he would have given to texts by Pound or Eliot. He enjoyed the stuff (or he didn't, as the case might be), but he also paid it the compliment (which its authors would often be happier to have remained unpaid) of critical attention — not in the blinkered, self-protective context of genre "criticism" as it then existed, but as though science fiction were an adult citizen of the Republic of Letters, responsible for its prose and its subtexts, not permitted the classic evasion of genre hacks that they're "only telling a story."

John's view of the critic's role was unconventional — or at least non-academic — in one other respect, since John also was ambitious to write fiction of his own. (He still is, and it is very good, but that is another matter.) One of the things that had prompted us both to take Patrick's *Quest for Utopia* class was that instead of writing a term paper for the course you could design your own utopia instead. I remember Clute's utopia at least as vividly as my own. It was a Borgesian prospectus for the world's most perfect and entire library. The underlying assumption was that nothing matters but books, their taxonomy and proper arrangement, and that the best society is that which most successfully achieves this end. I don't believe such conventional utopian issues as housing, family life, or garbage collection were considered even *en passant*. My memory may be at fault, and the actual paper Clute wrote might differ in detail. Yet it has struck me over the years what an uncannily prophetic account Clute had written. The perfect library of his paper for Professor Patrick was to take concrete shape over the years in Clute's own holdings and attainments, in the physical library he had amassed and the even more impressive mental datafile of all he has read, taken just estimate of, and remembered.

Readers who browse through *The Science Fiction Encyclopedia*, which Clute co-edited, if they take the trouble to note who wrote that volume's many critical surveys of individual sf authors, will be astonished at the sheer number for which Clute was responsible. No less astonishing is the range and judiciousness of his taste, qualities usually very much at odds in genre fiction. Happily, with the publication of this first collection of his critical writings it will be possible for readers who are less systematic than Clute himself has been at tracking down *everything* germane to a critical understanding of sf to have an opportunity to read what I consider the most far-ranging, authoritative, and sheerly enjoyable body of critical writing in the field.

Forward//

Early this year I went to Mexicon, a literary-track sf convention held on this occasion in Birmingham, in the dying compost of the Midlands of England, and a couple of the things that happened to me there it might be unoffensive to repeat. Most importantly, I met Jerry Kaufman, the co-publisher of Serconia Press, and we agreed on the spot with dreamlike speed to work together on the book I'm now forwarding. To Colin Greenland, the mutual friend who introduced us with *Strokes* in mind, I at least will remain grateful, on and on. Less importantly, because panels are always less important, I appeared on a panel with the shared remit to discuss something about the creative process, or maybe it was something about criticism and the creative process, or even criticism *versus* the creative process. I'm not sure I remember; nor am I entirely sure what anyone else — Alan Moore and Jan Mark and some others were there — had to say. Oddly enough, I retain some memory of what I said myself.

When I try to understand the creative process (I said) I often find myself thinking of the author Georges Simenon who, in a career extending from somewhere around 1921 to the present, has published way over a thousand stories, about 500 novels, and a dozen or so volumes of memoirs. Besides its delirious fecundity, what has most interested me in Simenon's career is a distinction he made for most of it between two kinds of novel — two kinds of writing which involved him in two varieties of the creative act. His secondary novels are the ones he is most famous for, the 70/80 books about Inspector Maigret; but it is the non-Maigret novels (well over 100 of them — we get to the 500 total only after including the 100s of pseudonymous books he wrote before he was 30) which have always meant most to him. Most of these primary texts follow a similar pattern. We begin with a situation of some rigidity, and a protagonist who is trapped in that situation. Something external, or something welling up within him, provokes a climate of extremity, a moment in which the protagonist is stretched to his uttermost, and breaks, or does not break, murders or does not murder his wife or mistress, flees or fails to flee. The novel then ends, often in a state of chaos: for the world when deranged, the psyche when liberated, crosses the borderline into the unknown, where habits no longer work, and reality, for an instant, may just possibly be seen entire, unendurable, profound and cold. The Maigrets are completely different. In these novels we *begin* in chaos, in the aftermath of some terrible breakdown in consensual reality; a murder has almost always been committed. Maigret appears. He senses the chaos and incompletion of the world, and within him something begins to knit the raveled sleave. Slowly, surely, intuitively, cognitively, implacably, he puts things together again. He finds (and forgives) the murderer. At the end of the novel he leaves the world like an egg (to quote one of Philip Larkin's most extraordinary poems) unbroken. For me, the process of writing a work of fiction can most readily be illuminated by the rage for chaos exemplified by Georges Simenon's non-Maigret novels; it is a process which has also been given theoretical substance by Morse Peckham in his *Man's Rage for Chaos* (1965). On the other hand, the art of writing criticism is the art of Maigret: it is an art of reconstitution, but also of closure; for in the critic, as for Maigret, there is a rage for order. Both the rage for chaos and the rage for order, though one may be higher than the other and more profound, are impulses of the creative spirit; and it is in this sense that I feel, when I am acting as a critic, that I am acting as a kind of creator. Accusations that the critic is inherently parasitical have always seemed fatuously self-serving to me, and it is with the countervailing sense that the critical act is a form of shaping that I allow myself the presumption of reprinting a few of the reviews and essays I've managed to shove into print over the past 25 years.

Three things have been done to these pieces. First, original typescripts have been used, rather than edited copy. Second, a few syntactical clumsinesses have been removed, but in the reviews no opinion, however stupid, has been given a hindsight edit. And three, I've inserted in unique brackets and dated [thus *1986*] some comments and second thoughts. Of the pieces included, the terminal essay on Gene Wolfe's *The Book of the New Sun* is entirely new. For the others, I have to thank the journals involved for the necessary permissions. More particularly, I'd like to thank, in chronological order, for their kind sharp wits and their sacrificial permissiveness: Michael Moorcock, Ed Ferman, Hilary Bailey, Mike Dirda, Ev Bleiler.

London/Florida/1986

1//Being Earthbound; or Toronto Tale

Late on this chill Sunday I walked south on Huron Street to Dundas, and passed a cold Volkswagen, and suddenly the sun shone from distant space low in the west, and its rays hit University Avenue and the glassy Shell Building there which did not topple but glowed infernally. And I thought, in my peajacket, staring, that I was of the first or maybe the second generation of us mortals to see so flat and so vast and so vertical a reflection on this curved Earth, third planet from the sun.

And I grew dizzy, and willed myself aloft above Toronto, for I had been reading much science fiction — and possibly for that reason the Shell Building and the streetcars and the sewers and the timid innovations of plastic, all seemed suddenly insubstantial and on close view as imperfect and plywoody as a mockup of a new vacuum cleaner. The whole spume of technological 1966 seemed a clay preamble at that moment, for I was physically risen, rising above Toronto till the world curved visibly, so that I left the air of this quack bubble and entered, out there in space with a clear view, into the maturity of mankind, some several years hence, by when this prototype of the real world, where we now live, will have been urged into the rococo and through-composed City of God of our science-fiction dreams, and man will go travelling.

For some day we will have left all this world behind and our descendants will be in command: but not us because we were born too soon and all we have is the Shell Building for our time travel. We were born too soon and will — or our offspring will — be thought of as mankind's last generation of children, mankind's last mortals. And always I feel cheated. I want to be immortal too, I want to have a computer network interfaced with my frontal lobe so that I can think, I want to be polymorphously perverse, I want to partake of the physical potential of my species but it looks like I was born too soon and I look about and isn't it all too incompetent and incomplete for words, our world?

About a decade ago I read a science fiction story by Theodore Sturgeon in *Galaxy*, and as I recollect it was called "The Acrophobe," after its hero, who was afraid of heights, terrified that he might tumble blackly to earth. So he kept to the ground, and was in due course contacted by a group of men who (as I remember the story) promised to cure him of his terrible acrophobia. They gave him an address where he went at the appointed time; he was led down a tunnel into a small chamber, and there he was drugged.

He awoke to a vibrating floor. They came to him. "We are glad we found you," they said. "You are the last to have been stranded by the wreck of your ancestors' ship. Your home is here, not down there on Earth, here in the ship." And they punched some buttons and uncovered a viewscreen and there, miles below him, he could see the cities and the whole of the Earth. He paled and choked in fear. "No, " they said, "don't be afraid of the height. You must realize that you were yourself never afraid of falling. What you were in reality afraid of was that the Earth was *falling on you*."

And the former acrophobe looked, and saw that they were right, that the great stifling heavy sphere of Earth was too close: too close: that it was *above them*: that they were too close to the alien planet. And I've been haunted by that story ever since, for I've taken it as a parable of our present condition: that we are stifled here in our own juices, and that this is not our home.

Which is why I read so avidly in the literature of escape, I suppose. Because this congenital and tiny world is falling on top of me. As I rose level with the sun above Toronto I said Lord make me waterproof, but I remain mortal. I remember very clearly how I continued to walk south on Huron Street going waesuck waesuck, how the world kept hitting my feet like tons of lead.

Toronto Varsity//November 1966

2//FSF1//Campbell/Green/Page/Read

As long as John W Campbell edited *Analog* you could still pretend it was really *Astounding* in drag, at dusk with the light behind her, if you squinted, and you'd swear the old girl looked all of 1940 again, just as fit as she ever was in the great days when science fiction bootstrapped upwards from a swamp of pulp, Aphrodite reborn as Hugo. More virginal than ice she was. In the palmy preWar days, when the genre could be defined as those prose fictions published under the name of science fiction in American pulp journals and ingested by a fandom, indeed it was Campbell who "blotted out the purple of pulp," as Isaac Asimov reminds us in his introduction to *Astounding: John W Campbell Memorial Anthology* (Random House, 1974; edited by Harry Harrison), and while he lived *Astounding* doppelganged *Analog* with the legend of a moment in sub-literary history whose nature seemed apprehensible, under a rubric, to a chosen readership. A Golden Age in short.

During this Golden Age, Asimov goes on, "writers lifted the field from minor pulp to high art" under Campbell's influence, a claim possibly more muscular than litcritical, and aimed more at fans in the paddock than at those who happen to read prose fictions, some of them generic — but then what better place for eulogies to homesick dreams of life as a secret garden than the rather freemasonical anthology under review, comprising as it does thirteen newly-written stories in honour of Campbell and his universe, by old Campbell authors, carrying on old *Astounding* themes, stories and avoidance tropes in some of the old *Astounding* styles. Campbell's world was manipulable, positivist, tangible, solvable, a dream of mastery very much like America's then; Campbell's protagonists, like America's in 1940 before John Wayne glued on a wig and became a bellhop, were seen as equals of greater gumption, not victims; heroes, not targets.

Neither Van Vogt or Heinlein has contributed to the volume, nor does Asimov's offering us what is apparently his final Thiotimoline gag do very much to commemorate the tone of his typical 40s work, even as self-parody with love, but otherwise the *Astounding* of that decade is respectfully homaged by several of its trademark authors. George O Smith brings back his *Venus Equilateral* crew, to what must be deliberately comic effect, as Don Channing and Walter Franks, after hearing a lecture on the obsolescence of vacuum tubes, trot right off to invent a matter transmitter with the help of some of the new thingumajigs, whatchewcallum transistors; Clifford D. Simak closes off the *City* sequence with the departure of Jenkins for the stars at last, giving the author ample excuse (as though he ever needed it) to mourn a chunk of *temps perdu*; Hal Clement adds a clean, affectless pendant to *Mission of Gravity*; and Theodore Sturgeon (who must be rather a trial) renders the blurb (as they say) inoperative and vitiates the point of the anthology itself by showing up with an ancient coy blooper of a tale that Campbell *rejected* in 1939 for falling between stools, and it still does.

These stories and symptomatic gags all share a low creative heat (and slight air of embarrassment) that seems to demonstrate how difficult it is for an author to recreate themes and modes he has cast off or outgrown, but more to the point demonstrates how ineluctably the gates of Paradise have slammed shut on this particular Golden Age. *Astounding* can no longer flare into the mind its fluorescent Can-do, Captain. The icy euphoria in the Garden, when all seemed new to the eye, when that which exceeded your grasp was putty in your waldo's, has turned into literary and cultural fugue, a sign of terror at the corrosive, dying, genre-dissolving century — for any one at any rate who tries to hold on as maybe Campbell himself did, which is another topic. So the weakness of these stories could signalize maturity in those who wrote them, you might claim.

Most of the remaining contributions come from authors whose careers took off in the broader shallower 50s, with *Astounding* a little past its prime, one magazine among others, but holding on, especially in the constant introduction of new series. Several of these are officially terminated in this volume. Poul Anderson shuts down his loose Polesotechnic League sequence with a dumpy and surprisingly disjointed story in which doubts are cast on the very episteme of robber-baron capitalism itself, though the issue remains in no doubt for Mr Anderson, and in which van Rijn shows his age at last; Gordon R Dickson duplicates the theme, imagery, strategies and protagonist of "Warrior," an earlier episode in the Dorsai Cycle, with a re-run at twice the length (and you rather wonder what Campbell would have done to all that fatty tissue); Harry Harrison supplies a Pyrran jeu in his later, offhand, jokier style, a style which just might reflect a touch of boredom with dinAlt, di Griz, et Cet; Mack Reynolds concludes his El Hassan series with a return-of-the-Dirty-Dozen-to-die-with-a-laugh episode in which the children of the original corps ready themselves to carry on saving Africa, crying Can-do, Captain! at underdevelopment (and Africans); and the best story in the book comes from Cogswell and Thomas, involving a literal transmutation of the Imperial Space Marines: it might very well be the only contribution to this anthology which could have appeared, unaltered (though there is a sexual note or two), in Campbell's *Astounding*.

It's obviously anyone's guess what in fact Campbell would have made of these etiolated remembrances of an era he never visibly abandoned, except regarding the Sturgeon item, where he seems to have made himself clear; a speculation comes to mind, however, that he might well have evinced a certain editorial discomfort with these stories, because they are slack, and because the elegiac note they share points to the contingent reality of that which they commemorate (and bury), and there seems no evidence to hand that Campbell ever thought of *Astounding* as a lucky contingency, or a moment of innocence out of the deflowered world beyond the gates. Collectors will want the book for its series terminations.

Conscience Interplanetary (Doubleday, 1974) by Joseph Green comprises a group of linked stories originally published in magazines and presumably recast, plus a coda written especially for the book to wrap up all the loose ends — all of which puts it very awkwardly, but as there isn't any decent critical term in the lexicon to designate linked stories originally published in magazines and presumably recast (plus coda), how else can you put it? [I retain this awkward formulation as a minor historical note. In 1976 when, with Peter Nicholls as General Editor,

I began to think about how to organize information for *The Science Fiction Encyclopedia* (1979), I came across A E van Vogt's term for assembled books of the sort described; and in the *Encyclopedia*, and in any other piece I wrote after 1976, the term *fixup* is always used *1986.*] Publishers usually call these things novels, but that's marketing not criticism.

As it stands, *Conscience Interplanetary* has more false climaxes than a tv-movie, though no commercials, and gives the the general efffect of rapid transit through a railroad flat. However, its stories do more or less conform to an initial premise which, promisingly enough, utilizes the axiom that when two cultures of unequal technology meet, the weaker dissolves in shock, viz. Earth's larger moiety. *Conscience Interplanetary* translates this premise to the stars, in a period of human ascendancy.

In Green's dramatization of this premise, the Terran hegemony has created a corps elite of "Consciences," highly educated professionals whose task it is to judge on the intelligence of alien species, and to protect them if they make the grade. If they fail the IQ test, as in "The Butterflies of Beauty," their planet will be opened to the developers, for systemic concerns, problems of ecosystem disruption, lie outside a Conscience's brief, as does the general conflict (implied in the initial premise) between nature and mastery. In Green's universe, as in *Astounding*'s so long ago, mastery over nature cannot genuinely be questioned, and boy-Fausts may shed the odd boyish tear over the solitudes they call peace: but they do not call a halt. Can do, Captain Faust.

In fact, when you look at the stories, it turns out that a Conscience seems to function mainly as a professional emcee, shoehorning his fellow homo sapiens into a position where their exploitation of an alien world can be agreed to by the aliens under threat, as in "The Decision-Makers," even though by Green's initial premise this agreement *inevitably* seals the fate of those aliens' culture.

The coda — tiredly written — makes much of a red-herring cloak-and-dagger conflict between the political party on Earth that supports the Consciences, and its opposition which calls itself the New Romans, and which plumps for unlimited exploitation of the stars. As the preceding stories have made it clear how very efficiently Conscience Odegaard (the protagonist) goes about satisfying any realistically imaginable technocratic lobby, the New Romans turns out to be a remarkably shabby straw horse, and a dishonesty within the fabric of this assembled book, for Conscience Odegaard, and his compliant female, are the true New Romans.

A new writer, Thomas Page, comes halfway to writing an excellent catastrophe novel in *The Hephaestus Plague* (Putnam's, 1974), but breaks down on page 109, where Part Two begins and so does lunacy. In Part One, impregnable fire-igniting roaches, unearthed by a quake, invade first Georgia and then the rest of the American Atlantic seaboard while Professor Parmiter and a plausible array of scientists and organizations (including The Smithsonian Institution Center for Short-Lived Phenomena) try desperately to find a way to stop them, with eventual success.

But this brings us on to Part Two, where the Professor's researches into the mysteries surrounding his *Hephaestus Parmitera* become still more obsessive and go literally underground, where he discovers in secret that the roaches, when bred and raised as a family unit (after some complex miscegenation), begin to exhibit telepathic qualities among themselves through the beads of bacteria formerly thought to serve them solely as digestive organisms [an interesting premonition of Greg Bear's *Blood Music 1986*], and soon enough these family units are forming English words, Indian-file. (If Time is the Territory, then chreods creep Indian-phylum.) En masse, these bacteria have a certain wisdom, it seems, and kind of remember the Flood. Eventually — feeling homesick and anyway beginning to burn the country down again — the roaches all return to the hole in Georgia from whence they erupted in the first place, Parmiter tagging along. Unfortunately, however, they leave him there, on the outside, like the crippled boy of Hamelin, and the novel closes with obscure hints that someone may be haunting that hole in Georgia, perhaps (one is led to believe) the sad Professor, who was never easy with people.

Rather a shame, all in all — as the first half of the book is intelligently mapped out, suspenseful, and absorbing, especially in the detailed entomological investigations of the strange bugs, where the author's careful emplacement of Parmiter as an eccentric researcher *within* an activated scientific enterprise is both plausible and a great relief from that old genre shortcut, the scientist as solitary tinkerer. So it's all the more unfortunate that Parmiter becomes just precisely that, down there in the cellar educating his telepathic meta-roach.

Clearly it's old Leonardo da Vinci himself in the flesh, there on the Berkley cover, head bowed gravely as he soars into space on his Renaissance wings; and clearly something pretty peculiar has happened to him, because the world into which he soars features spaceships, a green moon, a second green moon low on the horizon, and a turquoise sky in which stars are visible. It looks very much, and the jacket copy supports the supposition, as though *Mister da V and Other Stories* (Berkley, 1974) by Kit Reed, which this cover purports to illustrate, is going to be a far-flung adventure novel about Leonardo and how he was "yanked" into the near or maybe even the distant future; and won't it be exciting to see how the great universal man of the Renaissance copes with spaceships!

But *Mister da V* is not a novel. It is a collection of stories, most of which are only marginally science fiction or fantasy. One of these stories is entitled "Mister Da V." It is domestic fantasy (not adventure sf); it is set in the present (not the future); on Earth (and nowhere else); and typically of Kit Reed's early vein, it is told from the viewpoint of the daughter of the janitor whose fantastical contraption (as it were magically) brings Leonardo to the present (and not therefore through the viewpoint of Leonardo himself, nor has he anything to do with the travelling through time). The burden of the tale is a rather sentimental rendering of the total uncomprehension with which the janitor handles the irruption into his narrow, limited life of an active genius, though for most of the text we don't see Leonardo at all — he's kept locked in an upstairs room.

All this is perfectly clear. In no way does Kit Reed misrepresent her modest intentions. Any misrepresentation involved must remain with Berkley Books, whose decision to buy *Mister da V*, when their faith in what they were purchasing was so minimal, must stand as an intriguing puzzlement.

In her early stories, which *Mister da V* presents exclusively, Kit Reed works with considerable success to sensitize the formula-ridden domestic moralities commonly found in genre magazines of the 50s, in which protagonists tend to be victims, not terribly bright, often superannuated (or junior) members of bewildered family groupings (twins pop up rather often), and in which actions, almost any actions at all, tend to be treated as punishable hubris. Sometimes her efforts have a taming effect: "To Be Taken in a Strange Country" fatally softens Shirley Jackson. Some of the stories read as finger exercises for later, more ambitious efforts. More often, though, as in "Judas Bomb," she avoids the pathos traps that accompany any attempt to humanize this mode of the domestic exemplary, and you hear the genuine voice of human beings caught in a world whose seeming indifference cloaks malice. Berkley's advertising savants should have stuck to that.

The Magazine of Fantasy and Science Fiction//June 1974

3//FSF2//Barr/Harrison/Rossiter/Simak/Reynolds

From the thin red line of social scientists who buck Professor Skinner's dreams of manipulation for the good of our tabulas rasa, we learn that as human beings we sense and comprehend our world through an interlocking network of sets or conventions that pre-select input and shape output, in the same way a genre does — so that if only the world would stop changing, as once upon a time in Arcadia, we might live in a constant conformity to ourselves. For a deep appeal of the Golden Age, as of space opera, lies in the Lure of Homology: in the identity of self and world.

But as childhood passes so has the Golden Age, and our world is change on change unceasing, so that for those of us sane or unsaintly enough to tolerate input-violations (ie anything new), life is an unceasing savagery to the state of the self; indeed, so constant are all levels of change in the twentieth century that we scarcely know how it might feel to just simply be . . . .

Though we do read a lot.

Before the novel of mimesis died in 1914, along with the finest flower of our chivalry, its sanguine stance of openness to the world it claimed to mirror had long dominated prose fiction; rendering the world as it actually was seemed not only an attainable goal, but a moral one as well. But the roof fell in. Claims that human perception actually embraced and re-transmitted the true "reality" of the world could no longer survive our knowledge that we brought ourselves as tools to the job, and that ultimately the job was ourselves. Consequently, most significant non-generic fiction today deals in some way with that mutual opacity (or alienation) between self and world which killed off verisimilitude as a goal for adults, the only place mimesis still can be found au naturel being besteller or roman-a-clef porn, where it lies bareassed.

And most generic fiction, whether written or filmed, seems to have taken over a job handled by the novel for 150 years: the acting out of the dream of mimesis that self and world are mutually comprehensible: the creation of a world whose fundament is visible, mainly through the actions of the kinetic hero (me) who wraps things up. For despite its progressivist rhetoric, despite its thematic dealings with extrapolated futures, generic science fiction is a deeply conservative form, hence its appeal, hence its deep resistance to Modernist (New Wave) attempts at subversion.

Nowhere is this clearer than in space opera, where a rhetoric of outlandishness (anything goes on the other planet) operates within strict conventions of transparency, *pace* Delany, *viz.* Tubb. Transparent to his kinetic role so that we wear him like a foreskin, the hero is precisely what the plot demands, with no extraneous opacity of selfhood to gum up the works. Unencumbered by social feedbacks, his actions are just as transparent as his self — and as actions are also overdetermined, clear-edged, unquestionable and tyrannous. If the hero has amnesia (and he often has amnesia) this point is only underlined, for his inability to know himself is no permanent condition of being (as it is with the true me typing), but only a plot-trope soon to be unravelled, usually with a bang: for in space opera, self-knowledge attends, and is in fact identical to, knowledge of the true shape of the plot which is changing the universe; the hero's recovery of his memory confirms our nostalgic intuition that the universe, now transparent through the sesame of the unravelled plot, is precisely the very same thing as that discovered self of his. This is the Lure of Homology.

(Why else read space opera?)

Nor do the outlandish worlds the hero visits or inhabits turn out to be modernist or picaresque enclaves of existential dubiety, either. Just the opposite, for they too are penetrable. A conservative author will typically approach the problem of envisioning a new world (Tahiti or Trantor) by constructing a dramaturgy in which lines of power are made visible, after the Enlightenment belief that *energy is available*. Knowledge is power. In a space opera, control of these lines of power will illuminate the Lured world, making it comprehensible to the hero at the reins, and to the reader. The typical space opera outback is set up to make the Baroque architechtonics of central takeover and command as easy as possible: it is typically an authoritarian culture, with an homogenous elite; its lines of power narrow neatly and sanitarily to a small grouping at the top known to the hero, who (especially if he's an amnesiac) often turns out to be the final boss — the Sun King — the Alpha Male at the heart of the maze — in any case. In the space opera there is no quicksand of powerlessness, because the space opera is you.

Surprisingly, newcomer Donald Barr's poetry-filled, acerbic, linguistically foregrounded *Space Relations: A Slightly Gothic Interplanetary Tale* (Charterhouse, 1974) adheres rather more closely to the above delineation of space opera than many technically more straightforward efforts from veterans of the genre, while at the same time making nods to other universes of discourse. An administrator and educationist entirely new to fiction of any sort, Mr Barr is nevertheless clearly familiar with this genre, which he has refused to spoof or to undercut with intimations of existential dubiety and the like; his literate intensity has gone to increase transparency, not to subvert it. I'd adduce the secret of his success as being love.

Plump complacent John Armbruster Craig, interstellar diplomat, is returning from moderate success at the Betelgeuse Conference when space pirates capture his ship and sell him into abject slavery on dread Kossar where, refusing to service an old homosexual aristocrat, he's soon relegated to the terrible coal mines. After some rousing adventures, during which he saves the life of his beautiful, sexually avaricious owner, Lady Morgan Stanley, he's seconded to her bed, where his education as a kinetic hero takes a new turn of the screw, she being a sadist. Fear makes his penis rise: he's transparently fitting himself to take on the whole world. Craig and his mistress fall in love with each other, but after a year or so he discovers an ominous alien artifact in a cave, proof that there's an inimical civilization somewhere out there, and realizes that he must escape to Earth and start saving mankind; which he does.

On Earth, the new leaner tougher smarter more decisive Craig rises meteorically in the diplomatic corps while at the same time pushing through concordats to array homo sapiens against the enemy; he also introduces a resolution banning slavery. He eventually returns with plenipotentiary status to Kossar, where he had never revealed his actual name, not even to Lady Morgan, and has some more adventures in the course of reshaping the planet which had reshaped him. Slavery is abolished, and the Lady Morgan becomes his wife. Mankind is surely going to triumph. The book ends with a poem about sex.

In the Tannhauser myth, which this story retells (or so the dustjacket assures us), the hero gains the world (the Mount of Venus) only to lose his soul, good solid stuff to be sure. In *Space Relations* John Craig gains the world (a conflation of Kossar itself and Lady Morgan) only to find that it *is* his soul. To ensure the reader's awareness of this bit of Enlightenment good news, Barr twists the novel structurally so as to imbed Craig's period of slavery into a loaded flashback context; the consequent explosion into self-ownership, self-knowledge, great prestige and the present tense is so pointed a simultaneity as to be virtually didactic. Add to that the extroverted, imperial-we, out-front sexual shenanigans, which the author seems clearly to nominate as homology's binding-glue in his text, and the result is a joyous dream: in which you bite the apple and the apple remains whole.

The sex in *Space Relations* does come close to burning through the genre, but Barr implants it carefully, and the book holds together; Harry Harrison, on the other hand, shovels a lot of sex into his new space opera parody, *Star Smashers of the Galaxy Rangers* (Putnam, 1974), and it pretty much rips the book apart.

The first two paragraphs of *Star Smashers* pretty well sum up his line of attack, and demonstrate the corrosive effect of misapplied sex:

> "Come on, Jerry," Chuck called out cheerfully from inside the rude shed that the two chums had fixed up as a simple laboratory. "The old particle accelerator is fired up and rarin' to go!"
>
> "I'm fired up and rarin' to go too," Jerry whispered into the delicate rose ear of lovely Sally Goodfellow, his lips smacking their way along her jaw towards her lips, his insidious hands stealthily encircling her waist.

In the first paragraph quoted, we seem to be haring off on an enjoyable burlesque of — say — E E Smith's Skylark sequence, though Harrison could well have another writer in mind, or perhaps just preWar space opera in general — the sort of story whose Yankee hero (invariably Anglo-Saxon, invariably a genius level tinkerer-inventor straight out of the First Machine Age) invents a spacedrive-weapon-radio-waffle iron and flits off into the galaxy, establishing Man's supremacy among those good natives he does not kill by accident, and totally eliminating any bad ones who still survive.

Plot-wise, *Star Smashers of the Galaxy Rangers* follows this Skylarkian routine faithfully enough, and scores a good number of interesting points (though with affection) against its rightwing tendencies, its lunatic insensitivity to lifeforms (ie Jews) and lifestyles (social democracy, say) not found in small-town American circa 1930, and its outdated generic shortcuts in general.

But in the second quoted paragraph, something is already going a little sour. It would be very hard to deny that E E Smith's version of the American female is a misogynist's dream of intrusive fatuity, and that his heroines have dated even more badly than the plastic Edisons they natter at. All the same, however, it only travesties his kind of space opera, fatally distorting its nature, to transform his typical female ament (Sally Goodfellow in *Star Rangers*) into a sexual being, albeit a joky one. A good parodist would illuminate Sally Goodfellow's *lack* of sexual characteristics, but he would not do so by making her into something the heroes of the Skylark sequence (and possibly Doc Smith himself) could only possibly conceive of as a slut.

Introducing his *Parodies: An Anthology from Chaucer to Beerbohm and After*, Dwight Macdonald describes the form "as an intuitive kind of literary criticism . . . It is Method acting, since a successful parodist must live himself, imaginatively, into his parodee." The concept of the parody as a hostile review, insultingly couched, does not survive such familiarity with the form that Macdonald's collection offers, and it is here that *Star Rangers* shows a certain misdirected haste, diminishingly. Sally Goodfellow's intrusive tits are a fatal slip into burlesque editorializing; likewise her riposte to Chuck and Jerry when they claim noble motives for going off to war again: " 'Nuts! You do it for the old *machismo* . . . .' "

Sex also crops up in new writer Oscar Rossiter's *Tetrasomy Two* (Doubleday, 1974) (from that publisher's library list and you think they might have given him some good advice about that title), and we all have a reasonable amount of fun, though this amiable little tale, ill-balanced between its two main themes, does rather break down in the hokum apocalypse of its final paragraphs. In the main theme, which the author slights, a hospitalized human vegetable turns out to be an amoral, telepathic superbeing, who intends to eliminate the solar system in the process of gaining sufficient energy (and apparently karma) to visit his pals in Cassiopeia. In the secondary story, the superbeing telepathically forces his doctor's nurse into a state of sexual receptiveness; gratefully, the doctor, who perilously resembles Woody Allen in *Play*

It Again, Sam, gets into her pants, the world well lost. This takes most of the book, and shouldn't have. Muffled by lack of focus; otherwise a promising debut.

Predatory aliens out of early A E van Vogt invade Earth 500 years from now, driving mankind into the desperate expedient of returning en masse through time to the present, confronting the President of the United States with some serious logistical problems, for there are two billion of them. Informed by newspaper reporters and by his trusty radio of this incursion, the President discusses things with his Press Secretary, but is eventually gotten off the hook on learning that *Our Children's Children* (Putnam, 1974) intend to keep on going back through time, and have only stopped in 1974 to pick up some groceries. To pay for the goods they leave a few trillion dollars worth of diamonds with him — the USA being the only nation they can trust, cf. p. 185 — and prepare to disappear, along with the aliens, who are on their track, but who, being natural hunters, are much more interested in dinosaurs, and are therefore bound for a different time zone.

Thus Clifford D Simak, daydreaming through the afternoon of his career in one of the silliest and most absent-minded novels of recent years. His memorious readers will surely pick the thing up in search of the Simak we have all loved and admired, but they will find he has been sleeping. Some Prince should give him a kiss.

Mack Reynolds' *Commune 2000 AD* (Bantam, 1974) adds a few speculations on disaffection and the lust for power to his earlier and much finer utopian discourse, *Looking Backwards, from the Year 2000*, but finds himself trapped in the utopia format, leading to some pretty ludicrous plotting. He needs a naif to whom explanations can be made, and comes up with an academic whom the establishment sends off to the counter-culture communes in search of sedition. Each commune shows our hero a new sexual position, and imparts information to him that any child in the world of *Looking Backwards* would be familiar with from the age of five. Granted the utopia format requires a visitor (as from Porlock) who enters into dialogues with representatives of the ideal society, so as to illustrate its claims to "perfection": but Theodore Swain's skull is simply too thick to sustain life.

The Magazine of Fantasy and Science Fiction//September 1974

4//FSF3//Haiblum/Boyd/Eklund and Anderson/Ellison

Having clung this far to the century, we come to a terrain of salt flats, desolate marshes where the green revolution has failed and genres we have loved miscegenate in the slime like poleaxed dinosaurs, raddled by entropy and the death of ideology and the increasingly pyrrhic victories of technology against the planet, as a couple of the books on review may suggest, though not necessarily to their discredit, not necessarily. Still the center cannot hold and it begins to show. Harlan Ellison presents a clutch of newish stories that gnaw and nag, as usual, at conventions, taboos, coherence. Gordon Eklund joins Poul Anderson in, or maybe bamboozles him into, a collaborative effort that makes recent Van Vogts look positively *normal.* John Boyd grafts an sf ploy onto a Western format, which allows him to say something new, and quite possibly lunatic, about the old injunction to seize the day. Isidore Haiblum kind of tells four or five stories simultaneously within one novel, parodying hard-boiled thrillers in the process, and making certain other jokes as well. To label all these works as science fiction (or fantasy) is like calling the Holy Roman Empire Rome. Or Megalopolis Home. It is a marketing honorific. Nowadays it actually *sells* books.

Here and there in his new novel, *The Wilk Are Among Us* (Doubleday, 1975), Mr Haiblum does pay a kind of perfunctory lip service to the numerous sf conventions he judo-chops in passing with his speedy grin, but it's a dizzy ride all the same, this guaranteed comic romp, one that leaves the reader a little drained, a little sewered. Though Haiblum's spoofing of the aliens-are-among-us routines of sf never quite dissolves into the confidence tricks on our rights of expectation that it constantly threatens to become, there's still an uncomfortable sense of plundering to the book, a sense that its author has looted us of our rich, loving, ready memories of the conventions he quotes, and that he uses the energies thus purloined to fuel the jokes he plays on those very conventions.

Take the protagonist, for instance. *The Wilk Are Among Us* is narrated by a being whom the author would have us think physically resembles an octopus. But Mr Haiblum makes no attempt to construct a character for this being that would in any way distinguish him (it's a male) from any typical native-born New Yorker, and goes so far as to call him Leonard. Leonard Octopus? Perhaps that's a joke. Perhaps there's supposed to be a lesson behind it, that we're all really alike under the skin, which is a fine liberal lesson fictional New Yorkers are always embodying, one way or another. Unfortunately, what the actual text actually imparts is something altogether easier to put and less interesting to hear; under the skin, says Mr Haiblum's version of Leonard, we are all the *same*. What Mr Haiblum has neglected to invest his time in creating, consequently, the reader is forced to supply for himself out of that store of generic memories books like *Wilk* batten on: that is, some rudimentary, mind's-eye rendering of "Leonard" as the alien he's supposed to be, else the whole story collapses into that egregious whimsy science fiction authors are so prone to.

On assignment to a quarantine planet where socially hostile species can be studied in isolation, Leonard finds himself under attack by a potpourri of misfits from all over the universe, none of them described with any more care than he is — a brace of Wilk, a hunter, a nill, and a hairy unnamed creature who got there by mistake from another dimension. "I thought of screaming, pleading, and praying all at once," says Leonard Octopus, just like any other New Yorker you'd meet in an ethnic novel, though Leonard just may of course have three mouths and be able to carry it off. But the moment passes, we never learn any more about Leonard's capacities simultaneous-vocalization-wise, and soon become habituated to a style which speeds through solecisms like a newspaper article. Meanwhile, all four species, along with Leonard, are suddenly shot by his transmitter (a double-talk device familiar to any reader of sf action tales) in the twinkling of an eye to a totally unfamiliar different planet, which turns out to be Earth. Leonard soon discovers that his automatics (bits of double-talk which, being totally undescribed, operate whenever Mr Haiblum wants to get a move on) have turned him into a member of the planet's dominant species. Leonard now has hands. He has been turned into a Wilk.

Though not quite. The story begins to speed up here, aided by a (double-talk) translator and a (double-talk) computer-link to Leonard's home base called the Wizard. It turns out that homo sapiens are only sort of latent Wilk, which serves to add yet another species to the shambles. As none of the space or any of the (double-talk) devices are tied down to any working descriptions, the resulting noise is tremendous, and the general effect scatty. Transmitting, translating, Wizarding, and doing anything additional necessary, via his handy automatics, to move the plot without explaining it, Leonard FitzWilk (nee Octopus) eventually hares it through a hundred or so closely-similar episodes until he recaptures the various anti-social aliens. On the way home the reader gatecrashes a variety of story types, modes of narrative, characters human and otherwise, but is forced to quit them all (via transmitter or automatics) whenever there seems to be some point in remaining. And every once in a while he gets a chuckle out of it, does the reader. But he pays through the nose.

Genre-mixer John Boyd, on the other hand, homes in steadily to his zany climax. In his science fiction Western, *Andromeda Gun* (Putnam, 1975), a photonic nebulosity named G-7 visits nineteenth-century Earth, plants itself into a Western protagonist named Ian McCloud, and tries to puppet-master him into a state of moral rectitude. What a silly photonic nebulosity! G-7's inevitable fate is like that of any Nervous Nellie from Harvard who comes out West and John Wayne whups him until the True Grit hidden beneath those effeminate East Coast pinko ways peeps through that pansy flesh: seduced by the stinging vitality of his host, by the sight of genuine non-socialist human females in rut, by the sheer *gumption* of the phenomenal world, and by any number of other smarmy clichés out of Eric Frank Christopher Russell Anvil about how great it is to be a man, G-7 decides that what he should do with the rest of his photonic glow is, um, seize the day. Aha you say. Easy enough in theory, you say, but what can seizing the day really mean to a *bulb*? Simple. But first G-7 must quarantine the planet (piss off your hungry, piss off your poor) so that his fellow luminosity pinkos will have to stay clear, their lily-livered Harvard moral principles and their obsessive anti-free-enterprise concern for energy conservation and the like having made them incapable of grasping this seize the day stuff. Indeed, G-7 admits:

> . . . the ethereal race might be taking its righteousness too much for granted. Perhaps it had been force-fed precepts of harmonics and energy conservation that were not beyond being questioned. Possibly it was best that these human beings seize their revelry, live madly and upon the hour, then die.
>
> . . . Looking on itself from the viewpoint of an Ian McCloud, it could see itself not as a message bearer but as a celestial meddler, flitting from one star group to another to invest more forcible hosts and impose on them the dull conformity of unrelieved goodness, the ethics of conservationism, interfering in the free movements of mobile organisms which loss of entropy was bound to get, anyway, sooner or later . . . .
>
> . . . Seize the day, G-7 thought. Don't conserve it.

That done, the planet safe from conservationists, G-7 can then use nearly the last of its remaining light to flit back into the skull of Ian McCloud, determined to make his host into the best seller of moonshine liquor to Reservation Indians the West had ever seen.

Leaving aside the extremely odd notion that it's *loss* of entropy that causes the day to seize up in the end, because that may just be a slip of the pen, this quote still faces us with a pretty extraordinary declaration of animus against ecological or systems awareness (and hence against the real meaning of *carpe diem*), along with a covert but readily decipherable argument (couched in decrepit Goldwaterese) about man's inalienable right to ransack nature and to cheat other men because a man's gotta do what a man's gotta do. G-7 certainly gets off on the smell of the economy that's a free market for winners, a death-trap for Indians. Sentiments of this sort surely fuel the light bulb's arguments that consumption is all, its plumping for a universe in which to *seize the day* means to *confiscate the goods.*

Not that the book itself is totally vitiated by the arguments it purports to give flesh to; the story of Ian McCloud's bulb-induced transition from gun-toting outlaw to financial respectability based on *fun graft* buzzes on from scene to scene with commendable speed, writing savvy, and some wit. When ideology does rear its ugly head, however, not only does it offend comsymps like myself, but it also serves to terminate the story long before the plot's worked out. Once G-7 gets its revelation about the dubious ethics of conservationism in a man's world, we're forced to forget our involvement in Ian McCloud's rise to magnate status. And suddenly there's a sound of gas escaping.

Inheritors of Earth (Chilton, 1975) is an awful, awful book. There is no way of describing it without rewriting it. A chapter-opening quotation demonstrates the case. For the reader's convenience in this study session, each sentence has been numbered:

> (1)It was far too cold out here for taking a walk. (2)Alec had neglected to grab a coat when leaving the house and was now actually shivering from the chill. (3)The sensible thing, if he wanted to do it, would be to turn right around this moment and hurry back to home and heat and bed. (4)Sensible — yes — but he knew he wasn't going to do it. (5)Sensibility was a state of mind that existed far beyond his present ability to accept. (6)His feet kept moving — without conscious volition. (7)Each additional step was a separate and individual motion. (8)One — then another — and another. (9)And, all this time, the house dwindled farther into the distance.

Although Gordon Eklund and Poul Anderson are both credited as authors of *Inheritors of Earth*, I do not believe that Poul Anderson wrote this passage. He may be sentimental at times; his storylines may derive more from pulp and less from mythopoeisis than he (or his protagonists) tend to think; he may sleep at the wheel. But he does not wamble like a spastic turkey on a skating rink. As I do not know the work of Gordon Eklund solo, I'm forced by logic to posit its resemblance to drunken turkey tracks sight unseen, which may be unfair, but look at the passage. Look at the first sentence: is it too cold to take a walk altogether? or is it merely too cold to take a walk without a coat?: see second sentence. See third sentence: is it sensible to go back to the house whether or not he wants to go back to the house? or is it a "sensible thing" to do only if it's something he *wants* to do?: but see fourth sentence: no, it's not: sensible is sensible, period. See fifth sentence: sense and sensibility, as Jane Austen demonstrated in 1811 and as the dictionary established long before that, are not synonyms. Repeat: they are not synonyms, Gord. See sixth sentence: are we to remark on the presence of volitionless feet? or on the fact that walking had become solely a motor activity at this point?: not the latter: see seventh sentence: each step is "separate and individual," not simply a motor activity, therefore we *are* supposed to remark on the presence of volitionless feet. See sixth sentence: see eighth sentence: check. See ninth sentence: are we supposed to remark on the fact that the house is not *keeping pace*?

.End of paragraph.

See next paragraph (page 87). Alex gets out of sight of the house (it does not trail along behind him). It's a short paragraph. See next paragraph. For the third time in three paragraphs, the chapter begins.

See Gordon Eklund learn about stretching copy. See Poul Anderson spanking Gordon Eklund very hard, don't you just wish.

At the very minimum, science fiction books should wear a style that resembles newspaper copy in its transparency to content; ideally, science fiction, like other forms of literature, should work towards a consciousness of the ultimate unity of form and content, a consciousness we on our side, as readers, do our best to tune out when we're trying to surrender ourselves to baroque, highly machined stories of the sort *Inheritors of Earth* claims to be. A priori, then, we give to our reading of *Inheritors of Earth* a kind of willed innocence, a gift from us as consumers to Gordon Eklund and Poul Anderson as producers. And the least we can expect in return is a book that doesn't gobble in our faces.

The story proper seems to begin on page 97, with Part Two of the book. Though I don't have a copy of the March 1951 issue of *Future Combined With Science Fiction Stories* to check, I wouldn't be surprised to see that "Incomplete Superman," Poul Anderson's original effort, out of which this novel has been blown, begins at this point, and that all the maundering and shilly-shallying of the first half of *Inheritors of Earth* must be the responsibility of his collaborator.

Starting at page 97 then, which enables us to avoid Van Vogt Yaw in the process, Van Vogt Yaw being what happens when short stories are tossed into a novel and get seasick, we see that a superior stock has somehow been grafted onto homo sapiens, and plans to take over. Complicating the picture are half-breeds, all of them sterile, like mules. These half-breeds don't know of the existence of the pure stock, and think *they* are the coming thing. Everyone gets worked into a fine frenzy. There's a new religion, and a saintly android, and a few mere humans, and a beautiful daughter. There is also a telepathic gestalt, comprised of an assemblage of the aforementioned ingredients lightly stewed, which defeats one of the supermen in another dimension (yup) at what turns out to be a crucial moment, for it is the end of the book, resolving absolutely nothing but leaving one lonely omnipotent police officer with a ray of hope. It is not one of Poul Anderson's more characteristic tales. Fahrenheit 451 may solve the storage problem.

But Harlan Ellison provides a better bargain than usual. His new collection of stories, *Approaching Oblivion* (Walker, 1975), not untypically subtitled *Road Signs on the Treadmill Toward Tomorrow*, reprints nothing from previous volumes of Harlan Ellison short stories, repeat nothing. Only one of them — "Silent in Gehenna," already published in a couple of books — was familiar to me, to my misfortune, as I disliked it rather more the second time around. It's one of those stories whose climax is meant to have an admonitory, pistol-whipping sting to it, but which, in the event, merely jumps up and down and says *gaaaaaa!* Joe Bob Hickey is the last protester in a monstrous American police state. Everyone else is cowed. Apparently the cops are all there for *him*. He blows up a college or two and just before attempting to kidnap an adminstrative bigwig he's transliterated into another world or dimension, where he lives in a cage berating the aliens who own the place and who use him as a token conscience. This may be an allegory, but if it is, the lesson's too thick to slice. The reader fails to buy the self-pitying nudzhing *gaaaaaa* typical of solipsists trying to communicate ....

Other stories, notably "Kiss of Fire" and "Catman," enable Mr Ellison to focus his energies — they are very considerable indeed — into the depicting of worlds whose shapes are intricate enough, colored enough, bizarre enough, *realized* enough to provide verisimilitude for the kind of stories he likes to tell, the kind of protagonists he likes to infest them with. In these two stories, the dense knotty believableness of the surround drowns out any sillinesses in the plots, any tendencies towards primal *gaaaaaa*ing in the protagonists, and all's well, the darkness of the vision comes at the reader rifled, rather than blunderbussing about in search of a shape for itself, as so many of Mr Ellison's earlier stories tended to do.

Of the tales in *Approaching Oblivion*, perhaps only the last one, "Hindsight: 480 Seconds," is genuinely embarrassing. Earth is doomed. Vastator — readers of *Phoenix in Ashes* please note — is a huge wandering planet and is due to carom off the sun. Mankind as a whole has set off for the stars in huge ships, leaving just one poet, Haddon Brooks, to view and report on the devastation to come. He's a volunteer, one of ten thousand. He was selected because he was a poet. He composes a valedictory poem. "Vastator, the destroyer from the cold,/Eating time at fifty thousand kilometers per second," and so forth. He looks up and sees that the sky is blue. "I've never seen it so blue," he says. "Water, all the way to Heaven./But there are no birds." And so forth. He quotes one of poor sloppy Randall Jarrell's awfullest poems, aloud, by radio-link, to his wife. And so forth. When we come to his final utterance, just before the seas boil, Mr Ellison offers only a paraphrase, which may be the next best thing to being struck wordless altogether, but does not rescue us from having our faces rubbed into the fact that he is simply not a poet, is Mr Ellison, any more than most other other science fiction writers are poets, and that the idea of the poet as *lyric songbird* still queers some pretty sophisticated pitches, Mr Ellison's for instance. One black mark then, one or two *gaaaaaa*s, and some winners. You might ask for more, but of whom?

The Magazine of Fantasy and Science Fiction//October 1975

5//FSF4//Bester/Bryant/Harrison and Dickson/Herbert

The past twenty years in American sf seem to have housed a heck of a lot of apostacy, one way or another — uneasy departures into the grim, remunerative larger world outside, noisy reunions at conventions and conferences, everyone dressed in sheep's clothing for fellowship. It was just twenty years ago that Alfred Bester shot off into the night to hype for *Holiday* and other such organs — witness the despicably smooth-tongued piece on Asimov he includes in the second of his new volumes of collected stories — and just a couple of years ago that he made a large-scale though curiously insecure return with the serializing of what's now known as *The Computer Connection* in the States and *Extro* in Britain and, for all I know (he's always had trouble with titles), *Groupie!* in Hong Kong, a novel whose real genuine authentic Besterian protagonist (the possessed Indian scientist) is supplanted by a lame narrator who inflicts upon us all the new cliches of the recently dominant American Pals book, of which a bit more later. Perhaps as a professional writer Mr Bester was trying to accommodate himself to what he sensed was the mood of the day within the fold by chatting away at us in a pretty good imitation of a Samuel R Delany Paranormals Club Clambake — see *Dhalgren* for passages of American Pals psychic group-gropery at its squaggiest — but if so, the attempt proved nearly disastrous. The obsessive pazzazz of language and narrative invention that has always marked Bester goes sour in *The Computer Connection*, eats like spilled acid into the jumbled confusedly hectic tale he barely allows himself to tell, reeks of fundamentally displaced energies. Trying to charm, *Groupie!* devours itself.

Nor does the dedication — "For the fans — for the wonderful demented fans" — to the first of Mr Bester's two new volumes of stories (each ineptly titled) really augur very well, either, being too ingratiating by a long shot, too nice, too lily-livered, too entrepreneurial; a dedication like that has more the ring of a thank-you from the organizer of a clambake than of a message from an author deep in his devouring craft. Ultimately the trouble with this sort of posture on the part of an author lies in the way it can distort the relation between that author and his audience, often leading to an unvoiced, perhaps unconscious, certainly illicit assumption that the fan — that the fold — coinhabits the actual book and is part of its actual rhetorical voice. Sufficiently internalized, so that it trojan-horses the author's craft, this Session Fallacy is one of the strands that weave and warp together to make up the American Pals novel, with all its sins of unearned togetherness. [See Chapter 14 for an extended assault on the Session Fallacy, a term I may have generated, but may well — since it's so obvious a formulation — have not *1986*.]

Accompanied by generally informative, sometimes slightly smarmy, often hilarious comments, the stories themselves are another matter, most of them well-known from previous Bester collections and from anthologies, but welcome in assembled form. Unfortunately, however, the two volumes, though numbered consecutively, seem to have been conceived as separate endeavors. Each volume runs the same gamut of years, 1940 approximately to a year or so ago, but in neither volume are the stories arranged according to any principles I could work out. Lacking any chronological structure, therefore, Bester's comments have a scattier, more jumbled effect than they should have; the reader is forced to skip back and forth and from volume to volume attempting to give shape to the years. Doubleday's series (*The Early Asimov, The Early Williamson*, and so on) are a shining counter-example, and prove it's not impossible, or even very expensive, to make sense of things.

A list might help. *The Light Fantastic* (Berkley/Putnam, 1976) contains "Hell Is Forever," a long fantasy from 1942, exorbitantly and gratifyingly wasteful of ideas, and beneath the woodenness of its initial premise (the only sign of a newish writer) very Besterian indeed; then a batch of familiar tales from the peak period of the early and mid 50s, "5,271,009," which is one of a handful of genuinely funny sf stories, "Fondly Fahrenheit," "The Men Who Murdered Mohammed," and "Disappearing Act"; then a tiny, rather lousy by-blow from his 60s Avignon in the slicks, "Ms Found in a Champagne Bottle"; and "The Four-Hour Fugue" from 1974, an entirely competent return to the mode and concerns of the prolific years. *Star Light, Star Bright* (Berkley/Putnam, 1976) starts from go again, though not in any order, and includes "Adam and No Eve" from 1941, another story with a lot of woodenness and contrivance in its establishing shots, in this case (as I've always thought about this familar item) fatally, nor does the destruction of point-of-view consistency in the last sentence give off much of a thrill anymore; then a further batch from the 50s, "Time is the Traitor," "Oddy and Id," "Hobson's Choice," "Star Light, Star Bright" and "Of Time and Fifth Avenue"; then two singletons, "The Pi Man" from 1959, somewhat rewritten for this edition, generally to its betterment, and with a more open ending, as befits our emancipated times, and "They Don't Make Life Like They Used To" from 1963, whose contained hilarity plays so fruitfully on the repressed sexuality of the sf of the time that I found it still arousing, after a decade of private parts; "Something Up There Likes Me" from 1973, a rather frail sidekick of *Groupie!*; and some recent non-fiction including the dubious piece on Asimov already mentioned and a final autobiographical sketch, conducted with cheer and considerable tact, but without (nor has anyone the right to ask it) deciphering any tattoos beneath the skin.

Tattoos beneath the skin coerce most of the characters in most of the 50s stories, as they do in Bester's novels of the period. His characters are the actings-out of compulsive stigmata-bearing unconscious drives, of their tattoos. His view of man is autumnal, and much of Twentieth Century literature shares with him a point-of-view that is technically ironic, technically "superior" to its subject matter. Out of this common material and common import, however, Bester makes sf stories through a kind of sleight-of-hand: the worlds in which his characters operate are *themselves* radically shaped by his hagridden Gully Foyles and Oddys and the rest of them; dominating and coercing and obsessing the real worlds about them, they engender the situations by the binding extravagance of their natures. Simple enough, but heady in its implications, for this transforming of the internal into the external comes close to defining the deep structure of all genre creations. Understandably enough, most sf writers remain content with the vivid, entertaining, kinetic world of externalized dreams, where schizoid ex-marines remember their superpowers just in time to save the galaxy, and we're all American Pals together beneath the skin, jawing away. But Alfred Bester's peak novels and stories (most of the 50s batch in these collections) are different. They are passable excursions into the demonology of the self; and they are fine adventures in the light of day, Technicolor, torrential. More important than that, however, is the fact that their pyrotechnics work as an explanatory dialogue between the inner and the after worlds. For that reason — and because the man can write so well when he's not being a chum, or a posh journalist — they are about the best sf ever published. They define the genre they inhabit.

Edward Bryant presents us with his second book of stories, all in a row, chronologically ordered, the earlier ones quite brilliant at times, the later ones drawn and quartered by Killer Plot. *Cinnabar* (Macmillan, 1976) — the stories are all about a city at the end of time on the ocean by a desert in a dream of Southern California about as far from the reality of Southern California as Southern California is from the rest of us and in the same direction — kicks off promisingly with frissons galore, multiplex images and aperçus, half-seen and half-understood characters and episodes, marvels interbreeding with horrors, all mounting to a vision of the entranced plasticity of a life shaped by will and desire alone. In these earlier stories of the sequence, the nature of Cinnabar the city seems blessedly elusive; like life in a foreign realm, you catch ambiguously revealing glimpses of multifariousness — veils within veils — at the corner of the eye. There are a few coy-baroque tics, mainly the use of "cinematic" devices that stop the story dead while claiming to speed it up — freeze-frames, for instance, or lists that serve as an inept analogue of film cuts: The first thing Blank saw was (*cut!*) another Blank; the second thing Blank saw was (*cut!*) a razor blade; the third thing he saw was (*cut!*) a bleeding Blank. And so forth. But generally the first half of *Cinnabar* stands comparison with Bryant's earlier collection of stories, the brilliant *Among the Dead*.

Unfortunately the later stories — later both in time of writing and in the "history" of Cinnabar — flatten out disastrously, the horizon shrinks to the known, the plot thickens, becoming fatally explanatory, and a few chatty characters come to inhabit centre stage, where they set about *communing* with one another; it is here the vitiating over-gregariousness sets in, just as though the citizens of Cinnabar represented a not overly-imaginative *roman-à-clef* rendering of participants at a writer's workshop. Workshops are demanding and seductive experiences; one imagines a kind of rhetoric of community among their participants that both implies an external enemy (the cultural establishment, or the local police, or those who don't read sf) and grants an internal dispensation to cast off the trammels of individuation and *meld*, guys. External enemies make for strange bedfellows. When adolescents meet sf stars in heightened venues within the context of a genre that protects its own, maybe it's not surprising that American Pals stories flood the market with their easy optimism about the value of plebiscitary selfhood. Unsurprising — but deleterious all the same, because claims that community is attainable on the cheap, and that public confession of character traits absolves one of all consequent entailments and integrates you into a nest of chums, makes for bad fiction. In stories that expound or succumb to this oceanic fellowship, antagonism and tragedy are externalized, blamed on cartoon enemies (like the males in Joanna Russ's otherwise exemplary and moving *The Female Man*), while any differences within the group are "solved" by issue-dodging uses of paranormal empathy (see Vonda McIntyre's new novel), or telepathy, or sex, or shared stigmata, or nostalgia. When Tournaline Hayes and Obregon and Harry Vincent Blake make it together late in *Cinnabar* at enormous length, you can feel the author beginning to coast and tootle. You can feel the magical *difficulty* of Cinnabar dissolve into a series of routine variations on the theme that Intercourse is a Real Nice Clambake, as Snoopy the Eurovision Beagle might have put it. And you are ready (Nature abhors a vacuum) for plottiness to take over, too, so that by the time Terminex the Ultimate Computer *explains all* to the surviving indistinguishables, the complex vision Mr Bryant began with has suffered the death of paraphrase. A story that can be paraphrased is a lot of rote. It's a sad lazy ending for an author so amply capable of depths and shades beyond Terminex's terminal Eurovision patter.

— With my brains and your brawn, said Gordon R Dickson to Harry Harrison, I betcha we can write about the best space opera you ever read, and in three days too, numbskull.

— With *my* brains and *your* brawn, said Harry Harrison to Gordon R Dickson, I betcha we can write about the best space opera *you* ever read, and in *two* days, lunkhead.

And so the author of *Dorsai!* and the author of *Make Room, Make Room* got down to work, and ended up with *The Lifeship* (Harpers, 1976), a space opera. All brawn. Their model was an interesting one: Casts of interesting characters trapped in a lifeboat or on a magic mountain have made the careers of more than one neat playwright, neat hack, Thomas Mann. It's a model designed to make it easy for the microcosm (the lifeboat) to mirror and comment upon the macrocosm (the world). But it's the essence and joy of that model that it's precisely a metaphor, prismatic, potentially fruitful, tactful about the enormous gravity of the world it illumines. So it cannot decorously plot out as a bloody *conspiracy*. For when you add, to the microcosm-metaphor, characters in the "lifeship" we're about to monitor who not only metaphorically reflect the outer universe but also (for this is a space opera) have a very good chance of actually *changing* all of human society (the macrocosm) for starters, and the rest of the galaxy (which is the macrocosm as painted on the walls of the Slan Hut) for dinner, *then* you have an open field for the worst kinds of misplaced concreteness, with analogies transmogrified into *coincidences*, accidents of plot into the keys of the kingdom, and so forth.

Nor do Dickson and Harrison miss many doggone chances to cash in on this open door to hilarity and chaos. Every single character trapped between the stars in the lifeship seems to have at least one secret identity, two secret missions, three guilty deeds to atone for, four threats of death to dodge, five pear trees. Post-catastrophe Earth has become rigidly feudal, with Adelmen (nobles) and low-statured arbites (workers) making up society; why pig-German is used to describe them I couldn't work out. Adelman Giles blows up a spaceship operated by the space-dwelling Albenareth (Poul Anderson out of Tolkien) so that it will be forced to crash-land on the nearby planet where a rebel Adelman is hiding who wants to liberate the arbites right away rather than mañana, but an arbite on the Albenareth ship (he's really a cop in disguise) sets off a second explosion, forcing a select group of survivors into a lifeship — Giles; the secret cop; a clutch of conspiring arbites; and a couple of Albenareth, one of whom soon dies, leaving behind a pregnant female who goes into shock when a drug-crazed arbite eats her navigation manual for the cellulose (this coincidence, in which two separate species, one of them spacefaring, both use cellulose-based paper defies explanation and gets none), motivating Adelman Giles ('cause an Adelman's got to do what an Adelman's got to do) to dig real deep into that Gordon-R-Dickson-patented dark irresistible flaming never-say-die inexpugnable core of humanity that *always* distinguishes men from Albenareth and other alien breeds, and suitably roused he pilots by the seat of his inexpugnable pants the lifeship to safety on the planet he'd been aiming at in the first place, where all the conflicts between men and Albenareth are taken smartly in hand, so that the future looks rosy for both species at last. The whole farrago is narrated with a dead pan and a limp wrist; the two authors have done so much better on their own that one has to wonder just what six secret motives possessed them to write this thing, what seven deadly threats they used to get it published . . . .

It is early days yet to understand Frank Herbert, nor does *Children of Dune* (Putnam, 1976) go very far on first reading — the first of several, I suspect — to elucidate that sense of combined bemusement and exhilaration he can command through whole chapters — indeed whole books — of extraordinary opacity. Like *Dune Messiah*, though unlike *Dune*, this concluding volume of the trilogy is mostly talk — engrossing, infuriating, elusive, gnomic, inspissated, delphic, pregnant, self-absorbed *talk*; talk about the changing ecology and melancholy fate of the planet Dune or Arrakis where almost all the action takes place; talk about the Bene Gesserit breeding program and Jessica the Queen Mother who drops in to represent it; talk about Paul Muad'dib-Atreides who returns diminished from the dead as a blind anonymous prophet of decay and a gadfly of the Church established in his name; talk about his twin children Leto and Ghanima who are the novel's hidden protagonists (but who are never long enough together to become Pals); talk about his sister Alia who has become an Abomination (there does seem to be an unfortunate tendency throughout the trilogy for women to be punished for self-assertion, with poor Alia betrayingly described as "a gloating, almost masculine figure," and her guards as "amazons") and is consequently and Abominably possessed by the "ghost" of Baron Vladimir Harkonnen, volume one's main nasty; talk about gholas (from volume two), about loyalty, betrayal, palace politics, geriatric spice addiction, jihads, corrupt priests; talk about the slackening of the Fremen way of life as plants begin to bloom in the desert too soon — and all this talk couched in an arcane translatorese out of *The Prophet* (dam) by *Arabia Deserta* (sire). And all this talk is irradiated with the thought of decay, failure, mortality, loss, loss. Perhaps uniquely to sf, *Children of Dune* is a deeply and convincingly pessimistic novel about the impossible cost of attempting to master the universe and all that it inherit.

As in *Dune Messiah* a relatively clear-cut story does eventually emerge to summarize, perhaps a little vulgarly, everything that has gone before in talk. Alia has been declared regent of her brother's empire and jihad until the coming of age of Leto and Ghanima, both of whom, like Alia herself, were born sentient and in communication with their generic predecessors (see *Dune Messiah* for details). By now a Harkonnen tool,

Alia tries to destroy what she has been given to defend. Leto realizes that he must bite the bullet his father had "died" rather than face up to, arranges his own faked death, and goes into the desert of Dune to become "the Golden Path," the embodiment of an imposed, thousand-year, para-jihad imperial peace. He achieves this embodiment by merging his human nature and flesh with that of the sandtrout (the great sandworm's imago), acquiring super powers, and wiping the slate clean of the obsessive internecine past. As the novel closes, we know that the deserts will continue to disappear, that the humans whose fates and whose discussions we have followed for so long will become ancillaries to Leto's strange bleak regime, and that the myth of Muad'dib will be closed down. It is a sad close to the long dark epic, but somehow very bracing. Tragedy is that.

The Magazine of Fantasy and Science Fiction//February 1977

6//FSF5//Varley/Hoyle/Van Scyoc/Ashley/Disch and Naylor

Sometimes, reading a novel, one is able to play a game with the thing. Disregarding the ostensible date of the narrative, which may of course be anywhen at all, one can try to estimate the *real decade* in which the story is set. This *real decade* will be the period most nearly reflected by the book's characters in their feelings about the proper relationship between the sexes, for instance, or about the threat of international communism, or about how great an economic sway should be exercised (across the galaxy) by entrepreneurial capitalism, or about the inevitablity of man's victory over the stars in their courses. No book whose argument assimilates progress with mastery over aliens can be really set after the Viet Nam War, for example. It is of course a fundamental rule of this game that no sf novel (nor anything at all in our world) can be *actually* set in the future; from that subtends a further rule — that the closer a book gets to the real present the harder it was to write, to read, to understand and to appreciate, rather as though the present were analogous to the speed of light. And it is a fundamental read-out of the game that sf novels tend to be set much further into the real past than most "mainstream" non-generic novels. After all, sf *is* generic writing, composed, marketed and read according to laid-down expectations regarding form and content. Generic writing tends to resist innovation; absolute generic writing resists innovation absolutely.

Through the infinite universes of the "tomorrows" of sf gape the fixed stigmata of the genre's last assimilated novelty — Heinlein's, or Asimov's, or Dick's, or Delany's.

Or Varley's.

A comparatively new writer, John Varley has already been compared to Robert A. Heinlein; like Heinlein in his early stories, Varley, in his first novel, *The Ophiuchi Hotline* (Dial Press, 1977), abruptly updates the sf genre's treatment of its material, and like Heinlein in his time he does it without seeming to revolt against the field in which he's working, or the readership he makes no sign of holding in contempt. In no way does *The Ophiuchi Hotline* transcend its origins, the way Thomas M. Disch's books do, for instance; if Varley's novel is revolutionary, it's a palace revolution. In fact most of the themes it deals with are common fodder to most writers working in the 70s, whatever the *real decade* of the books they turn out. In *Hotline* there is a good deal about the moral and practical entailments of cloning, for instance. There are two sets of aliens with whom humanity must somehow deal: the Invaders who have banned man from Earth; and the humanoids who have been secretly operating the Ophiuchi Hotline itself, a sort of information service beamed in from beyond Pluto somewhere. There is a Nivenesque elaboration of Inner Planet-Asteroid Belt conflict in lifestyles and politics, and a Haldemanesque garnishing of excerpts from relevant documents, letters, reports and the like. As the Invaders have given man the boot for the sake of all Earthly cetaceans and now inhabit Jupiter, there is some routine mysticism about the fifth planet, along with gassy speculations as to the Nature of Intelligence. There is a great deal of extremely casual sex, much of it unfortunately recounted in that tone of detumescent fellowship so popular with the current crop of writers. As human opposition to the Invaders is controlled by a man named Boss Tweed, there is plenty of sf's rote cynicism about civilian politicians, too. Taken out of context, nothing in *The Ophiuchi Hotline* sounds as though the book were going to add up to much more than more of the same (garnished).

Put into the frame of the storyline itself, however, these clichés begin to look a bit different, and the book begins to show its worth. Having been exiled from its home planet, mankind now lives in artificial warrens in the Moon, Mars, and anywhere else possible in the wainscotting of the solar system, which is routine enough, except for one catch: When the novel begins, man has already been in exile for 500 years, and as we continue to read, we begin to see — with a series of curious shocks of recognition — just how thoroughly he has adjusted to his new "urban" existence amongst his life support systems in his fluorescent tunnels. Nor is that all: Well before the end of the book, it becomes clear to us that man's exile is permanent, and that he will never be permitted to return to his home habitat. The 500 years of exile have been deeply traumatic, of course, but the traumae have been healed, with the aid of the Hotline, which for centuries has been disseminating the scientific and technological data necessary to make human life palatable in its enforced hidey-holes; *Homo sapiens* has adjusted to its new econiche.

The book's protagonist is a woman (and it is another element of novelty that she can be used as protagonist without any excuse-making or self-preening auctorial comment), a geneticist who as the story begins has been condemned to genuine death for illicit experimentation in human genes. She's taken the illegal precaution of having herself cloned, however, and so has Boss Tweed's revanchist conspiracy, which needs her technical skills; one of the Lilo-clones owned by Tweed is therefore substituted for the real — or at any rate the first — Lilo, and is executed in her stead. Cloning in this book is a double operation, however: The body may be sf's usual Hollywoody one-sac identical, but the mind is a topological read-out of the original's mind as of the date when mapping took place; when needed, this read-out is remapped onto an awakened body. The catch is, of course, that the new Lilo will be as fully an adult human being as the original Lilo, minus a few weeks or months of post-mapping memories, and will be just as desperate to stay alive. The execution of the clone-Lilo, in the first pages of the book, is therefore savage and moving and very horrible. And this effect is only sharpened a bit later on — one cannot help but think of Hitchcock's *Psycho* doubled and redoubled — when, after she baulks at Boss Tweed's incarceration of her for his own dangerously quixotic ends, the original Lilo is also killed off and replaced by a clone. This clone *also* rebels. The Lilo who eventually gives in and with whom we spend most of the rest of the book is several Lilos removed from the Lilo we began with. Nor is that all: The original Lilo's own surreptitious clone, subjectively younger than any other Lilos (because she was recorded earlier), is also active in the Asteroid Belt, and a third active Lilo-protagonist is created when the "main" Lilo falls into Jupiter to her presumed death — though in fact one of the mysterious Invaders translates her to Earth, where a few humans are allowed to survive without technology, and there, away from youth-maintaining drugs, she begins to age. Each of the three Lilos takes on protagony in turn through a series of deadpan, curiously shocking transitions — shocking because we're used to a more liberal, individualizing, perhaps more archaic treatment of human identity than Varley allows us; this being one of the ways in which he is genuinely modern, of course. More broadly shocking, however, are the reactions of those who know these various Lilos to her/their abrupt rebirths and to the ignorance of later versions of events and relationships more recent than the mapping which made her/them possible. Most everyone has sex — it is called copping — with everyone else, but because Varley's is a different world from what we have learned to expect in sf writing, abrupt terminations and transitions of relationships are neither surprising to his novel's characters, *nor are they dehumanizing*. Cloning and copping and living in tunnels in permanent exile and breathing stale air and using the Ophiuchi Hotline are *not* innovations for the characters of this book. Time and again their calm acceptance of an environment radically (if at times unconvincingly) different from our own expectations brings home the novelty of the book in the sf world, and its author's resemblance to the early Heinlein, because both authors create characters integrated with the environments they are described as living in. Like Heinlein's, Varley's characters are deeply competent with the world they know. And if Heinlein's Future History is a series of rewritings of 1935, and shocking at the time for fingering the inner bone so close, then Varley's deracinated urban exile from irrecoverable roots reflects the 1970s through the dance of clichés of genre, likewise.

The story's close underlines the depths of sorrow we seem to feel in 1977 about the world we have so irrecoverably lost. *Homo sapiens* turns out to have a very weak claim to the real estate it's mucked about on, and the second clause of the Invaders' eviction notice is about to become operative: We are now due to be booted from the solar system itself, and to become, like as it turns out the Ophiuchi humanoids, homeless interstellar wanderers: Fieldmice. Self-recognition causes vertigo; Varley seems to be telling the truth about the species. But because the book is a genuine piece of generic sf, the three Lilos do undergo, all the same, in the midst of all this desolation, a vaguely Kubrickian epiphany-of-self-recognition routine, do come to easy new understanding about themselves and mankind, and do prepare to face the stars together, as cheery as Podkayne. As a marriage of genre solipsism tropes with American Pals lovenestery, this narcissistic ensemble of Lilos will take some beating. But the taste of exile remains. It is certainly 1977.

The Fred Hoyle Band sticks to the old faith, however, presenting us with a new chase caper, *The Incandescent Ones* (Harpers, 1977), whose *real decade* can't extend much past 1950. Though alien humanoids have landed on Earth with offers of cheap power and technological assistance, and though 200 years have passed since they did so, the world of this novel is still wracked by Cold War conflicts, cars and trucks have changed not a whit and still use petroleum-based fuels, and young Peter, an American exchange student in Moscow, undertakes an undercover mission for the American secret service (or so he thinks) with no more fear of consequences than Dave Dawson ever showed when defeating General Rommel with only Freddy Farmer to help him along. The chase extends to Turkey, where young Peter's meant to deliver to someone or other an alien super-battery. En route he finds out, with total aplomb, that he's not human at all but in fact one of the monitoring humanoids; this impassivity on young Peter's part is eventually explained, in the book's one coup, by the fact that he and all the humanoids are actually robots created by the mysterious incandescent ones who live — guess where — on Jupiter, the In Planet this year. That Peter's a robot seems to be a comment on the requirements of this form of paranoid space opera, as witness most Keith Laumer protagonists — but there is absolutely no evidence that the comment is deliberate on the Hoyles's part. Young Peter (an expert and nerveless skier, unsurprising given his absence of nerves) soon finds himself slaloming across the electromagnetically-enhanced reefs of space surrounding Thus Spake Zarathustra, and the novel closes with his arrival at the residence of the incandescent ones, who absorb him into their "vastly greater awareness." The book reads like the recounting of a dream, and its changes of venue and perspective are markedly dream-like — it's only too bad that its crew of authors and Barbara Hoyle (who edited) couldn't spare a few pages to dwell on their creation.

Sydney J. Van Scyoc's *Cloudcry* (Berkeley/Putnam, 1977) starts off with promise but soon flounders into a narrative impasse, where it remains for 150 morose alliteration-choked pages. Afflicted with an incurable, highly contagious disease, human Verrons, and bird-descended Tiehl are marooned by the Authority on a quarantine planet, into the depths of which they soon duly plunge against orders to discover all sorts of ruined cities and at least three distinct species of intelligent being. How the Authority could have missed noticing all this garbage neither Verrons nor Tiehl (nor Van Scyoc) think to ask, enmiring themselves instead in a mesa city, where Tiehl reverts to avian savagery and dreams of having wings again, and Verrons (along with an equally sick chum) falls under the thrall of the energy-devouring *flutes* that when blown reactivate the extinct flying people of the planet (making a sort of fourth species). Blowing these flutes has the effect of turning Verron (and his chum) into the most torpid of idiots, and as it takes most of the book for them to discover that they have been turned into the most torpid of idiots, and the rest of the book to get clear of Mesa City, *reading* about blowing these flutes turns the reader into something like jelly, too. True, Tiehl's reversion is graphic enough, as is Van Scyoc's comparison of his state with that of a planet-bound descendant of the flying people, named Aleida. But the bulk of the book is as exhausted as Verrons (and his chum) are. Eventually Aleida gets a jewel to fly by, and flies off (has anyone ever remarked on how closely opened wings resemble yawns?), and Verrons (etc.) find themselves cured of their incurable disease, and hightail it off-planet just as fast as they can, having come to their senses. Most readers will have used their exit visas long before.

Bad stories don't necessarily make a bad anthology if its editor is trying to make a point, nor can good stories save an awful one like Mike Ashley's atrocious little money-spinner which he calls *Souls in Metal* (St. Martin's Press, 1977) because it's about robots, and because (I guess) it would be hard work (not his forte [a stupid thing to say on the basis of one bad anthology; and in numerous ways Mr Ashley has since demonstrated the fatuity of the utterance *1986*]) to find a robot story that *didn't* say something by commission or omission about robot consciousness, robot souls, robot compunction, robot um sense of humor .... Not one story in the collection could have required more than a modicum of research to uncover. There are warhorses by Asimov and Harrison, Leinster and Simak, Kuttner and Dick and de Camp. There's Lester del Rey's hilarious "Helen O'Loy" (1938), that famous crazy-comedy romp complete with female robot who commits suttee when her human husband kicks the um bucket and many other wry ironies which the pre-war sf community apparently thought comprised a movingly sentimental description of the ideal female. But Mr Ashley neither reads it as deliberately (or unconsciously) loony, or an offense to half his potential readership; he merely calls it "what is still considered the most important yet ... story about a female robot," and drops the hot potato. In general his editorial comments are among the most illiterate ever printed, with high-school syntax howlers and unintended neologisms breeding together (see page 36, line 13) like fruit flies in Hiroshima, nor on decipherment is what he says about his assemblage of stories even interestingly *false*. Maybe Mr Ashley can't write book

English, and maybe his publishers don't know what book English is; I think it's more likely, however, that in slamming together this jalopy of a book both editor and publisher were thinking of other things than mere quality of product — that neither of them were (as Mr Ashley might put it) totally unbeknown to thoughts of the ensuant buck.

Utterly different is *Strangeness: A Collection of Curious Tales* (Scribners, 1977), edited by Thomas M Disch and Charles Naylor, latest of a series of anthologies beginning with *The Ruins of Earth*, each one of them expressing a sustained argument about the world, an argument buttressed in each case by a meticulous assembling of material, perhaps most obviously with this current offering, whose contents run from Philip José Farmer's beautiful idea badly developed, "Sketches Among the Ruins of my Mind," through Graham Greene and Virginia Woolf and Thomas Mann (though his story is seriously disappointing) all the way back to Sarah Orne Jewett. The argument of *Strangeness* is hard to put, and Disch finds himself in some difficulty putting it. At the heart of Edgar Allan Poe's strange monomaniacal art — Disch seems to be saying, though locating this essence "in the blood-dark depths of the heart, or even deeper, in the soul" is simply and lugubriously to word-spin — lies a confluence and mutual refraction of soul and landscape, through the signs of which gape like stigmata not the tricks of genre but the etiology and arabesque lineaments of Kierkegaardian alienation in a world bereft of God; and the stories collected in *Strangeness* derive from the Poe of that reading. I suppose I find some difficulty in putting it too. Certainly the death of God marks a significant absence in most of these tales, for most of them are shaped as contemplations of the taste of the fate of being human in the Western world, and into the mirrors most of these stories construct there stares a dreadful solitude. Shirley Jackson's contribution, and Joyce Carol Oates's, M John Harrison's and Pamela Zoline's, all inhabit a *real decade* long after the failure of the centre to hold; they are stories in which our tools fail and our souls hallucinate and we are for the dark, and our efforts at surveying, as in Brian Aldiss's brilliant "Where the Lines Converge," only serve to demonstrate the essential wrongness of the human condition. So it's a pretty grim book, in its way. Little of it is sf, not much is fantasy; most of these stories are too *solitary* to permit genre trappings, which assume a shared transparent world. Most of us read genre fictions to escape our solitude. *Strangeness* returns us to reality.

The Magazine of Fantasy and Science Fiction//1977

7//FSF6//Delany/Yarbro/McIntyre/Dozois

First a personal note. As a reviewer of sf, here and elsewhere, I've been accused of pedantry, bias, logorrhea, bile, sophomoric obscurity, and some other things. These accusations are accurate. They have the ring of truth. They can be sustained by chapter and verse. I mention them in order to register my knowledge that, when I take a few digs at Samuel R Delany's criticism, as I'm certainly about to, I'm going to be accusing him of sins I've been amply guilty of myself, though of course never again.

The book in question is Delany's collection of critical essays and reviews called *The Jewel-Hinged Jaw: Notes of the Language of Science Fiction* (Berkley, 1978), or so the subtitle reads in Berkley's revised and corrected version of the original 1977 Dragon Press production; presumably some of the corrections are more felicitous than changing *Notes on*. . . to *Notes of*. . ., though grammatical, stylistic and factual howlers do still abound, despite Delany's paying of thanks — "for myriad microimprovements" — to three colleagues, whose names I thought were oddly spelled. But when one actually experiences the clotted preciocity of his prose, the phrase quoted above being entirely typical of its uneasy condescension and agglutinative gumminess, then the multitude of typos and other errors does seem more forgiveable, because translatorese is always hard to get a grip on; the Rube Goldberg *unworkableness* of much of the writing in this book, especially in the earlier and middle essays collected, does in fact make the task of winkling out paraphrasable content almost impossible. Trying to do so I got vertigo and eyestrain and began to drink heavily over the three months. Ultimately I failed, as the three microimproving colleagues must have before me. I could not even patch together an adequate sense of what I had failed to understand; after all, as Delany does say in a clear moment, style and content are intersecting models of one another. I'm paraphrasing him. At the heart of this failure of mine — beyond the word-deaf gaucheries of the style, beyond the intrusive self-congratulatory garish foregrounding of the auctorial voice with all its morose cheeriness and duckpond aggro — lay a sense that when I *did* think I understood the terms and assumptions shaping a paragraph, by the dint of a lot of deconstruction work, what I was left with was a kind of shambles strewn with disqualified data and beheaded arguments, a spastic *Guernica.* An example is overdue. The one I'm going to pick — because I'm not going to try anything really hard — is couched far more clearly and calmly than much of the book. It is from a 1968 essay on Thomas M Disch and Roger Zelazny entitled "Faust and Archimedes," though the meaning of that title kept dodging out of sight down webs of semantic branching. Part of the argument of the piece is designed to show that although neither writer would fare badly when compared to the "mainstream," the very idea of a mainstream of literature was of little use when the best innovative work of the likes of Disch and Zelazny makes nonsense of a distinction — mainstream vs genre — which is in any case invidious. A few years earlier, though — Delany suggests — in the late 40s and 50s on up to about 1957, the work of sf writers like Leiber, Merril, Pohl and Knight *could* unfortunately be described in terms of these genre authors' relationship to a mainstream in the doldrums:

> . . . For the most part the narrative techniques [of stories by Leiber Merril etc] are naturalistic. What was being produced in the mainstream at the same times as these stories were being written? Early Capote, the first novels of Mailer and Bellow, the last books of Hemingway, the tales of J D Salinger, Faulkner's *Snopes* trilogy. All of these are remarkably staid works. The most experimental would be Kerouac's *On the Road* and even that looks downright classical compared to the literary experiments of the twenties, thirties, and early forties: *The Sound and the Fury, As I Lay Dying*, Dos Passos's *U.S.A.* . . . Borges' fables in South America [. . .], Genet's criminal peons in France (so many people forget that *Notre Dame des fleurs* was first published

> in 1942). It is actually a little depressing to realize just how closely the best s-f of that period does parallel the mainstream. But the parallel justifies the critical concern. All this writing was done before *Catch-22* or *V.* Though Durrell and Nabokov had been favorites of a small coterie of writers that, admittedly, included figures as diverse as T S Eliot, Edmund Wilson, and Henry Miller, their names were almost unknown to the intellectual public. Neither Barth nor Barthelme had published.

So. It's a pretty tendentious list of the "remarkably staid" that Delany presents us with, nor is it by any means clear what his criteria of inclusion were — some of the books and authors mentioned were popular at the time, some later; some are American, some are not; some mainstream, some not; and so forth. As a list, then, which had better be accurate as far as it goes, and as far as it goes had better be pretty thorough, the signs are already ominous. But let's take a closer look: Norman Mailer's first novel, *The Naked and the Dead* (1948), is certainly not experimental, nor is it really very staid, but his second, *Barbary Shore* (1951), is decidedly experimental (though kind of staid). The first volume of Faulkner's *Snopes* trilogy, *The Hamlet*, was published in 1940, and is neither experimental nor staid; the second and third volumes, published in 1957 and 1959, are not experimental but are indeed extremely staid. On the other hand, of Faulkner's publications that actually fit into the period the list is supposed to describe, *Requiem for a Nun* (1951) and *A Fable* (1954) are both highly experimental (and very staid). His early work, like *The Sound and the Fury* (1929), was initially appreciated by a rather smaller "coterie" than that which already knew of Vladimir Nabokov when he published *Bend Sinister* (1947), experimental (and not staid), or *Nine Stories* (1947), some experimental some not (some staid some not), or *Lolita* (1955), not staid, or *Pnin* (1957), calm (but not staid). It is somewhat deflating to realize that "Genet's criminal peons" are most probably not law-breaking members of the laboring classes of South America on a European prison tour, but are merely criminal paeans, and if we find that "so many people forget that *Notre Dame des fleurs* was first published in 1942," it is probably because most people who are aware of the date of its first publication know it was first published in 1944, and that in any case Genet's most intense creative period lies in the decade after this date, as does the beginning of his influence on the "mainstream." The same might be said of Samuel Beckett, whom Delany doesn't mention, but whose published works in this remarkably staid period include *Watt* (1944), *Molloy* (1951; trans. 1956), *Malone Dies* (1952; trans. 1956), *The Unnameable* (1953; trans. 1958), *Waiting for Godot* (1952; trans. 1954) and *Endgame* (1957). But one should be fair to at least one version of what the list is supposed to describe, and if one sticks closer to North America than Delany does, a list of authors relevant to any look at innovation in the novel at this time should include Malcolm Lowry with *Under the Volcano* (1947), John Hawkes with *The Cannibal* (1949) and others, Bernard Malamud with *The Natural* (1952), Wright Morris with *The Works of Love* (1952) and other books before and after that one, William Gaddis with *The Recognitions* (1955) and James Purdy with *63: Dream Palace* (1956). All experimental. Some staid. Some not staid.

It is certainly the case that Kerouac's experiments in *On the Road* (1957) pale beside the accomplishments of the great Modernist writers who mourned the end of civilization in the 1920s, but lack of interestingness does not make a work "downright classical," unless by "classical" one means, ah, *staid*. Right. Got it. "Classical" means old-fashioned. *There's* an argument for ya. But enough (John Barth published *The Floating Opera* in 1956) is enough. It's enough to demonstrate that in this case (and others) the data upon which Delany bases what seems to be an argument can be so amateurishly skewiff that after you wipe the gouache out of your eyes there's nothing left but unbalanced and indecipherable assertion, and what that assertion is designed to demonstrate *I do not know*. I will reiterate a confession. I have spent all this time in the bilgewater because I don't know how to describe the ship. All I can say is that some idiot savant has had this craft on the rocks somewhere, because the bilge is rising.

But that's not entirely fair. Bits of the arguments about the nature of sf as opposed to "mundane" literature, though tendentious and embarrassing in their attempts to restrict the imaginative scope theoretically realizable within a "mundane" text, are at least arousing. And the late long essay on Ursula K Le Guin's *The Dispossessed* (1974) is a brilliant demolition job. Delany is at his best when he's forced to stick close to a given text, and his close reading of Le Guin interestingly foreshadows his most recent work, *The American Shore*, a book-length structural analysis of a short story from Disch's *334* (1972); I have only seen unbound galleys of this book, however, and will not presume to deal with a work of its formidable complexity on the basis of an uncorrected and unpublished text. The Jaw is open. May it close on meat.

Three book-length fictions here. Ah call them novels why not, even though only one of the authors involved, Gardner Dozois with *Strangers*, actually expands his original novella into a tale of sufficient complexity to warrant its new length, while Chelsea Quinn Yarbro, with *False*

Dawn, and Vonda N McIntyre, with *Dreamsnake*, merely extend their original (and both excellent) short stories (McIntyre's "Of Mist, and Grass, and Sand" deserved its Nebula) into shambling quest tales whose episodes append themselves to that original material like rows of dominoes, both writers only laying off their task when enough words have been written to make up the length (though not the substance) of a book. There's no need to go over the exigencies of a market that favors short stories and pays relatively little for the product it favors, while reserving its really substantial rewards of cash and fame for book publications, however arrived at. And Yarbro and McIntyre can hardly be *blamed* for responding with no more than strictly professional decorum to the challenges presented by their own material, though at the same time neither of them can be much praised for skating, however decorously, into a sow's ear.

But still. But still. Both Yarbro and McIntyre have (perhaps unconsciously?) attempted to bluff their way down a very difficult course indeed. To use a short story as the first chapter of a novel means that the meaning of every word of that short story must be radically altered. The words that make up the narrative of a short story comprise a resonating insight whose closure (with the last phrase) completes a vision the mind's eye can hold entire; but when those exact same words make up the narrative start of a novel, a transmutation occurs: Sentences in the short story that move to aesthetic closure become, in novel dress, a series of establishing shots *opening* us into the multifarious complexity of the longer form, into a vision the mind's eye tends to examine as an interwoven mosaic. A continuum. Of course sf writers tend to optimism about the form of the novel, tend to assume that there is no significant difference between an interwoven mosaic and a row of dominoes, between a *novel* and a *quest*. Hence the proliferation of fixups. As a consequence, sf writers have become used to creating worlds subject to constant magical transitions, gaps, manipulative reality shifts, all of which can be seen as an expedient technical presentation of the sf sense that the given world is inherently subject to radical change. Perhaps that is why the message underlying so many of the cheapjack fixups that proliferate so wantonly is that the world is easy to change. If you have a magic carpet at hand, why bother with a mosaic?

But still.

Something has to happen. In "False Dawn," the short story that serves as the first chapter of *False Dawn* (Doubleday, 1978), a tough but nervous female protagonist is managing to survive a vastly complex ecological disaster that has engulfed and ruined the world; she treks through a grotesquely Boschian California, her survival facilitated by a mutant capacity to regenerate her own tissue, and teams up with a one-armed man who turns out to be the ex-leader of a vicious band of marauders who seem to be attempting to cleanse the land by killing off mutants, destroying farm communities, and spreading their seed in rape sessions; indeed, Yarbro's protagonist is herself savagely raped, and finally escapes into the night with her companion to face a future that can only be desolate. End of short story. Because it *is* a short story, the rape of the land and the rape of the lady model each other effectively, and her final escape is closure indeed, and a false dawn. In the full novel, or domino patch, the story continues with the protagonist trekking across California with her companion, hither and yon, searching for a safe haven in the raped land while torturing herself with images of her personal rape. Within the texture of the extended tale, these images fail to resolve, despite an extraordinarily perfunctory sexual coupling she finally permits her friend. At the end of the novel — after the effective marriage of versions of rape has lost all its shaping power — the two of them once again escape the marauders, but with as little hope as the first time. The story has been demolished, and nothing has taken its place. We are where we began, after a lot of words have turned the resonances into plod. Nothing has happened. But the book reads easily, makes no challenges, has only one difficult word (agapate), can be slept through comfortably, and will be popular.

Vonda N McIntyre's *Dreamsnake* (Houghton Mifflin, 1978) turns out to be set in the same desolate future Earth as her first novel, *The Exile Waiting*, though to little effect. In the short story, the wandering healer Snake has lost her dreamsnake, an alien serpent whose bite soothes the dying into an easy demise; the tale of how this loss comes about is a moving vision of incomprehension and blindness, a vision whose strength lies in the sense that the loss it depicts is irreversible. In the novel it turns out not to be irreversible at all; Snake treks across her world, doing a bit of healing now and then, adopting a daughter, and questing for a new dreamsnake. Knowing that her society of healers has gotten its snakes from an underground city (that of *The Exile Waiting*) in the middle of the desert, she goes there, but is superstitiously rebuffed. But all is not lost (there are pages to fill). Discovering that a half-destroyed bubble dome harbors humans who own dreamsnakes, she goes there and after some travails acquires not only a passel of dreamsnakes but also the secret of how to breed them on Earth. Meeting

Arevin whom she loves (from the original story) she begins the journey home. One snake may be lost; a cornucopia of new snakes is found. Things are looking up for Snake. Tragedy has been transmuted into a picaresque ramble. It is the Death of a Thousand Dominoes. A sequel is anticipated (by me). Staid.

Gardner Dozois' *Strangers* (Berkley/Putnam, 1978) is something different, an organic expansion and elucidation of material rather than its mechanical extension through page after page of indefinitely prolongable quest routines. Several centuries hence, homo sapiens is permitted to travel to the stars in the ships of more advanced species, with devastating consequences to our mental health, as we've found ourselves to be a Third World race on a Third World world. On the planet Weinunnach, where Dozois' beefy, stubborn, psychologically blinkered young protagonist finds himself, Earth has constructed a sterile enclave from which its citizens attempt to conduct trade with the native Cian, whose complexly ritualized and fail-safed culture they make no real attempt to understand. Except for Farber, the protagonist, and Ferri, an ethnologist: the latter professionally; Farber because he falls in love, after a fashion, with a native woman. Although they are strangers at heart to one another, Farber obsessively strives to bind her to him, as though to cure the fundamental accidie of his species by a transcendental act of communion, so as to understand another person, so as not to be Third World. But it doesn't work. After forcing a marriage with her, and having himself genetically altered by the Cian so that they can interbreed, he tries to go native (in the enclave, Cian are self-defensively called Niggers) with her, but disastrously misunderstands her nature, and the shape of Cian culture, when he decides to have a child with her as soon as possible. Cian women die in childbirth. The secrecy of the culture has prevented knowledge of this basic fact from spreading, and Farber and Ferri only slowly come to understand the nightmare they have entered, the depths of nescience in which they swim. Before coming to a final knowledge of his ignorance, Farber in a tantrum of panic and denial bars his wife from the ultimate rituals designed to soothe her dying, so that she dies in the greatest of agony; his coming to awareness — however partial — is too late. She is dead. He has a litter of six Cian children. As the novel closes, he is looking for a male Cian to wetnurse them.

The novel form of *Strangers* tells the same story as the short version; what is new or augmented is a dense, detailed, almost sociological accumulation of data, both cognitive and sensory, to the end that the reader lives in the humid, hallucinatory presence of the ultimately alien and strange. This complex impaction of information — this interwoven mosaic — is what a novel can offer, if a novel has been written and not a game of dominoes. Dozois has written a novel.

The Magazine of Fantasy and Science Fiction//January 1979

8//FSF7//Crowley/Elgin/Carr/Zebrowski

Time does pass. After twelve months of novels that stuck to your shoes like dwagon-dew, 1979 has been a year it was a pleasure to review the books of, mostly. Arthur C Clarke and Frederik Pohl and Thomas M Disch and some others have put out titles near the top of their various bents, and, in the sequels he apparently intends to produce, John Varley may manage to pull *Titan*'s socks up a bit, if only in retrospect, though you do have to wonder — more and more his women protagonists are beginning to sound as though they came out of *recent* Heinlein, and the doting gigantism of *Titan* does seem to bring out an elephantiastic gormlessness to the way the story is actually told; but of that more later on, when we attempt to deal with George Zebrowski's *Macrolife*, a title which sounds like, and a book which has the texture of, a new brand of linoleum, battleship grey, dead permanent, though there is one thing that can be said immediately to its credit. No dragons.

And then there's John Crowley, author of *The Deep* (1975) and *Beasts* (1976) and of nothing else, who has just published his finest novel to date, and in the dark close warmth of its imprisoning integrity one of the best novels to yet come out of the sf genre. The integrity of *Engine Summer* (Doubleday, 1979) begins and ends with the title. At first glance a slightly irritating play on Indian summer, by novel's end it has become not only the meaning of the book but — complexly — the book itself, for ultimately we come to see that the very text of the book — the first-person narrative of its protagonist, Rush that Speaks — is precisely an engine summer.

Like *Beasts*, to which it is a kind of thematic sequel, *Engine Summer* is set in a post-holocaust America, though in this case so long after the event that pre-collapse humans are referred to as angels (but without approbation), and Indians have been so long forgotten that the glorious days of early autumn, during which much of the story takes place, are referred to as engine summer. Set in the midst of the long diffuse tedious terrifying collapse of technological Faustian man, *Beasts* is damagingly plotted around the kind of technophilic revanchist conspiracy that makes up the narrative substance of far too many American sf novels about our Balkanized future after the roads fail. The America of *Engine Summer*, in contrast, seems to be a kind of paradise inhabited by a series of ecologically modest oral cultures deeply attuned to the natural world; there seems to be no alienation.

Born into the Palm cord of Little Belaire commune, Rush that Speaks grows up obsessed with the notion, entirely proper to his culture, of becoming a saint. In Little Belaire terms, a saint is an individual man or woman whose life is a tale of such transparency [like Smoky Barnable's in *Little, Big* (1981) *1986*] that others can hear the truth of the world through its telling. Painted Red, his mentor, tries to explain: Saints (she says)

> are saints not because of what they did, especially, but because in the telling of it, what they did became transparent, and your own life could be seen through it, illuminated.... And in transparent life, the saints hoped that one day we might be free from death: not immortal, as the angels tried to become, but free from death, our lives transparent even as we live them: not through a means, you see, like ... truthful speaking, but transparent *in their circumstances*: so that instead of telling a story that makes a life transparent, we will ourselves be transparent, and not hear or remember a saint's life, but live it: live many lives in the moment between birth and dying.

In Little Belaire, an oral community the telling of whose dead saints' lives comprises the very warp and woof of all history and meaning, words are deeply important, and "truthful speaking" lies at the heart of those strings of narrative (or cords) that maintain social comity, for how else can the lives of the saints be seen through? As are all members of his particular cord, Rush that Speaks is an intensely dedicated truthful speaker, but for him to radiate that saintly transparency through which others can hear themselves be human, he must lead an exemplary life. *Engine Summer* is that longing. Is it exemplary?

After the girl he loves disappears one spring with the clan of roaming preachers called Dr Boots' List, Rush eventually follows her into the outside world, which seems almost as pastoral as Little Belaire itself. He hibernates with Blink, a saint of no fixed cord; he treks southwards, coming across the List's home base, where he finds his love, but she's strangely transformed, impassive, translucent, seemingly unconscious of the passage of time , for when she receives once a year, as do all members of the List, a "letter" from Dr Boots, the world begins afresh for her. He manages to receive a letter of his own; it turns out to be an epiphany; a strange glowing ball from the time of the angels briefly possesses him, prefiguring his ultimate destiny and infusing him for a moment with his love's translucently inhuman acceptance of the unchanging garden of the world. But he is troubled in his heart. A letter from Dr Boots is more like a lobotomy than an infusion of sainthood. He has lost her.

So he has to leave. After further adventures, he discovers an angel-crafted silver hand, which the tales of the saints have always spoken of in significant conjunction with a glowing ball of transcendant potency. Almost immediately afterwards, the dreams he has experienced of angel cities in the sky are confirmed when a genuine angel — alerted as it turns out by his discovery of the lost hand — parachutes down to him through the air, and the novel begins to close in on the deep pathos of its underlying premise. The angel, whose name is Montgolfier [after Joseph Montgolfier (1740-1810), inventor of the first hot-air balloon in 1783 *1986*], explains to Rush that the hand he'd discovered is a device (or engine) for the control of the glowing balls, which are themselves engines for the imprinting and subsequent replaying of entire personalities. Before humans had been first recorded, however, experiments had been thought necessary, and the ball that magicked the members of Dr Boots' List into recurrent rebirths had been experimentally implanted with the personality of a cat named Boots. But now Montgolfier has an offer to make, that of immortality. The floating angel city is in desperate need of an exemplary human personality to remind its inhabitants of their original nature as the centuries pass. Montgolfier offers to imprint Rush that Speaks' current state of human selfhood into a permanent glowing transparency. Though in the realm of time the human Rush that Speaks will himself live on, an aging mortal on a quest for sainthood, he will also have been transformed or doubled into a sentient playback in the heavens, and will remain in the heavens forever, a glowing ball in a silver hand.

The story we have read up to this point in *Engine Summer* is of course precisely that sentient record's tale of longing; this story is framed by a conversation we only now begin to understand, for it is a conversation between "Rush that Speaks" and a deeply moved listener, and it is taking place 600 years after the events "he" has been reliving through the act of relating them, just like a saint. These events, which comprise the life and memories and goals of the young Rush that Speaks, the "Rush that Speaks" within the glowing ball reiterates with precision and truth, as "he" has by now done on at least 300 occasions. Being at heart a recording, "he" begins each session anew, as for the first time, and on each occasion learns what it is "he" has become, only to forget this knowledge upon going to sleep again at the end of the tale. No matter how often told, this life and the words of its retelling remain paradigmatic. They are nothing but truth. They can be seen through. "Rush that Speaks" has become a radiance — a saint — through which generations of angels learn the meaning of themselves.

But for reasons the novel makes complexly and amply clear, the warm pastoral garden of a world "Rush that Speaks" describes is not an engine summer merely because, after all, a kind of engine is doing the job of re-creation; it is an engine summer because the world so lovingly described is precisely a contrivance of autumn, a dying Arcadia, for the cultures that make up this idyllic America are now scattered and dwindling, and human fertility is only precariously maintained through limited supplies of an angel powder; and winter is nigh. 600 years on, *Engine Summer* is only a text. And that is its ultimate truth. Typically of Crowley [for the end of *Little, Big* is also a death-march *1986*], the final revelation of truth turns out to be a demonstration of control. As in all his work, peace and solace are no more than cat's-cradles in the fingers of a huge closed hand.

Rarely in sf (or elsewhere) will form and message cohabit as powerfully as they do in *Engine Summer*; what you run across far more frequently, in anything more ambitious than pure adventure or escape, will be a defensively philistine scattering of material, so that the whole leaks its parts. Take, for instance, Suzette Haden Elgin, who wrote three novels about a decade ago, stopped for a while, and has now returned (it is, all in all, a welcome return) with a fourth book about Coyote Jones, her intergalactic secret agent. *Star-Anchored, Star Angered* (Doubleday, 1979), like its predecessors, boasts a good deal of razzmatazz, but simply cannot contain itself. Once again, impertinent sloppy huggable Coyote — mind-deaf in a universe where telepathy is normal — hares off on a planet-changing mission for the Tri-Galactic Intelligence

Service which employs him mainly for his immunity to thought-control and for his capacity to project coercive thoughts onto great masses of telepaths simultaneously. This time it seems that a female messiah-figure has cropped up on the planet Freeway, and is disrupting the rigid hierarchical faith that has up to now controlled the planet. Coyote's mission is unclear, and in the event he accomplishes very little, nor is he actually on stage for much of the novel, which as a consequence leaks anecdotes like a sieve [it may take a workaholic genius like P G Wodehouse to construct, as he does in any of the full-length Bertie Wooster tales, a novel most of which is hearsay recounted to us with utmost clarity by a narrator who never understands the point till the story's over, and to do this without creating a lumpy-gravy text raddled by anecdotes ineptly contrived to tell the narrator what he's got to tell us: but perhaps one shouldn't blame Elgin for not being able to emulate the legerdemain of the most highly skilled constructor of plots this century has yet seen *1986*]; which can dampen your pleasure. Coyote's main accomplishment is to fall deeply under the influence of Drussa Silver, the new Messiah, who soon performs some genuine miracles and who, like the revolutionary divinity she is, sacrifices herself to the powers-that-be, which gain only a pyrrhic victory in killing her, as our grief-stricken protagonist is told by letter at novel's end; this letter also informs him — for he has signally failed to understand (or indeed *do*) anything up to this point — that he'd been sent to Freeway not to investigate a spurious sect but to help kill a god (his help was unnecessary). The Three Galaxies (he's told) have cultures based (like Italian cities) upon a continuing competitive disunity, and could not tolerate the unified universe Drussa's genuine divinity might well impose. Nevertheless (concludes the letter) *chances are* (though we're not to find out) that Drussa's faith will triumph, and that Coyote Jones's cartoon dingbat universe will become an ecumene.

In bits, Elgin is a sharp, intelligent, witty, interestingly speculative writer. She has depicted Freeway's conflicting cultures absorbingly, though through a confusing variety of points of view (rarely Coyote's) [once again, Wodehouse shows how the job can be done *1986*]. Coyote himself has a warm heart and a beard. The feminism underlying the story is cogent and quiety sustained. But none of it much matters. Nothing has any follow-through. Because she has paid vanishingly small attention (or so it must seem) to the actual prime task of creating a fictional shape to transmit her various themes (which include the effects of a divine being upon an entire Three Galaxies), and because her protagonist (who must have bored her silly) is no more than an emcee (generally shorn of notes), what we're left with is gossip. (Gab.)

Best sf of the year anthologies must be terribly hard for anyone to assemble with a straight face. Titles like Terry Carr's *The Best Science Fiction of the Year #8* (Del Rey, 1979), in their attempts to convey a sense of the newsworthy and the canonical at the same time, give off an air of somewhat decadent pixillation, though I doubt Mr Carr could be accused of a lack of due sobriety in his performance of the task of selection, nor has he forgotten to include in Harlan Ellison (does he ever?). In fact the selection is extremely safe indeed. Most of the stories come from reliable (not to say canonical) sources; there are three from this magazine alone, and three from *Analog*. Included out should have been the Ellison, perhaps, as "Count the Clock that Tells the Time" is one of his lesser efforts, professional enough, but slightly padded, slightly absent-minded, couched in a confessional mode but the confession doesn't seem to be his. The title is great but (as he acknowledges) it's Shakespeare's, and it doesn't fit the story. But Ellison (as a name anyway) is a sign of establishment cloth, and the rest of the anthology follows suit, though John Varley's "The Barbie Murders" is a dimly inconclusive question-begging word-spinner, and Thomas M Disch's "The Man Who Had No Idea" is unaccountably genial and without formal bite, so that a potentially formidable idea gradually declines into doodle. Ian Watson's "The Very Slow Time Machine" is crushingly metaphysical, like a ziggurat, or Barrington J Bayley; Gordon Eklund's "Vermeer's Window" manages not to be philistine about Vermeer; Gregory Benford and Marc Laidlaw's "A Hiss of Dragon" posits an interesting fake-dragon technology, but the story ends before it has properly begun. Fritz Leiber's "Black Glass" is one of the three best selections; a further installment in his series of confessionals about an elderly man haunted by alternate versions of America's destiny which infiltrate our modern world and darken it, the story will benefit from association with its fellows, but has a crafted elegiac clarity in its own right. "The Morphology of the Kirkham Wreck" by Hilbert Schenk recounts, in a tone of intense repertorial objectivity, an episode of time manipulation under stress, set in nineteenth century New England. Donald Kingsbury's "To Bring in the Steel" makes big business in the asteroid belt sound like something out of Richard Condon, but Richard Condon's strength lies in the animus he bears against the corporate world state whose pornotopic icons he makes glow like a Giger alien, and Kingsbury is a booster; nevertheless the story is nifty and bigger than life and you can get off on it. And that's about it; the anthology gives off a sense of time being bided in the pantheon, or maybe even time being bided by Terry Carr. Maybe there was nothing else better to print, but the narrowness of the base for selection, with six magazines or anthologies providing the entire contents, and the familiarity of most of the authors, does give rise to a desperate (but not serious) suspicion.

We come to *Macrolife* (Harpers, 1979), big, dense, terribly illustrated, dumb. And if George Zebrowski is as humorless as the prose he fills the marmoreal solitude of this book with, then he's not much of a smiler. *Macrolife* — the title comes from Dandridge Cole's vision of vast artificial communities whose cells would be "individual human beings, plants, animals, and machines" — is certainly nothing if not serious. And because it deals with important (not to say gigantic) issues, viz. humanity's future as we outgrow the planet of our origin, then perhaps the book *should* be inflexibly serious and didactic, deadpan, aspiring, solemn, sanctimonious, deceased. Pooh.

No way. It doesn't wash. If a novel is going to display a high-toned Stapeldonian seriousness about the next trillion years or so, there simply cannot be any pratfalls — humor yes, unconscious slapstick no — and so there can be no excuse for a plot as lamebrained and off the point as the one Zebrowski has riddled his vision with. Although the book is supposed to be about the macrolife interstellar "maturity" of mankind after we have left mere planets far behind us and have become cellular units in a higher transhuman consciousness housed mainly in hollowed-out asteroids and the like, most of the actual text is stupefyingly devoted to the misadventures of members of the Bulero family who, like the Beverly Hillbillies, are very rich, very unintelligent, and everywhere. Long ago the first Bulero had invented bulerite, a magical material that has become essential to all human technology and architecture on Earth by 2021, when the novel begins, with a great catastrophe. Bulerite is beginning to dissolve all over Earth and civilization is ending. The Bulero clan leaves Earth for a hollowed-out asteroid they had nothing to do with constructing. The dissolved bulerite begins to coalesce. Soon the planet looks like the egg of an orc. And that's that: Earth dies to get the Buleros into space, and we can forget all about bulerite. Zebrowski certainly does. A thousand years pass in the twinkling of an eye, but there are still Buleros around. Young John Bulero — clone of the dullest of the earlier Buleros — goes native on an alien planet in a sulk because he doesn't like his macrolife asteroid, and — because he is thick-witted and utterly humorless — manages utterly to destroy the culture he has visited himself upon. This takes up much of the remainder of the book. Then many billions of years pass. John Bulero — who else — is reconstructed from the elevated mass-mind of macrolife to save the universe by exercising his indomitable human will and guiding all the assembled macrolife containers through the ultimate black hole that ends our universe and into the next cycle. He is successful of course. The novel ends with a solemn peroration about macrolife.

The bulerite catastrophe and the John Bulero pratfalls are both narrated through a haze of extraordinarily repetitive propaganda for macrolife (the word itself must appear at least 500 times). Unfortunately, nothing in the novel works to dramatize these arguments, nor is Zebrowski capable of envisioning his higher plane of existence in terms that bring us [in *real decade* terms *1986*] much past 1960. When, for instance, he describes his hollowed-out asteroids, he makes them resemble nothing more (or less) than enclosed shopping malls, complete with Muzak; he may well *like* enclosed shopping malls complete with Muzak, but at a time when John Varley and others have developed a language for describing gigantic artifacts huge in scale and involvingly complex in detail, the enclosed shopping mall is hardly an exhilarating model for elevated speculation about the shape of our future. It's what you might call an Eisenhower high. Right. Macrolife would have been heaven for Ike.

The Magazine of Fantasy and Science Fiction//April 1980

9//FSF8//Reed/Schochet and Silbersack/Killough/ Benford and Rotsler/Malzberg

Let us speak briefly of the classic American cinema. Let us make the point that you can always recognize a Hollywood film because it *means* so much. This point once made will soon lead us to Walt Disney, and to Kit Reed's new novel, *Magic Time*, which attempts to dramatize the fascist mentality with a kind of light appalling brio, and which does not mention Walt Disney. But first. Because of the studio system which thrived in Hollywood until Lucille Ball got pregnant, it was possible for those in charge of making films to rigorously predetermine almost every detail of every scene that went before the camera to be translated into dream language, so that not a word, not a prop, not the veiled insinuation of a single tit, not an angle of lighting, nothing could be anything but *meant*. If the camera focused on a vase, on that vase would turn the plot, because there could be no vase for vase's sake in the Hollywood film, no vase that uncovered the face of God in an instant of ungovernable epiphany, *no mere vase* [the reference here being to Wallace Stevens's last poem, "Of Mere Being" *1986*]. The vase that remained was all meaning, use, story [No fire-fangled feathers dangling down. *1986*]. What we saw on the screen (and in these latter days, choked with nostalgia, watch again on television) was an intensely sanitized, chaste, debugged tourists' paradise, where it was impossible to get lost, where menu (to talk philosophical for a moment) preceded existence.

This being true of the Hollywood product, then the Hollywood filmmakers themselves, at least in their dreams, must have been veritable gods of those little worlds of theirs, in which the Tablets of the Law actually worked, and from which chaos was banished. The main difficulty, of course, must have always been people. Actors. The anarchic complexity of the human face must often have deranged the most rigidly prescribed Tablet or menu in a flash of Hepburn, and it's surely not accidental that the archetypal Hollywood mind (though perhaps not personality) was Walt Disney, the man who created, as an industrially-viable alternative to the subversive human actor, the feature-length cartoon. Nor can it be entirely accidental that Disney, having created a closed universe of meaning for Snow White, went on to conceive of Disneyland, which is a closed universe of meaning for the rest of us, at least in theory. If the world were Disneyland, who then could doubt the existence of God?

This is surely not an original point. It represents no radical new analysis of the human condition as imprisoned by Hollywood genre engineers (it might be noted that science fiction, speaking of genres, boasts a few engineers of its own) in general, and by Walt Disney in particular. Disneyland itself has become an honored part of the American nightmare of self-analysis, an immediately recognizeable emblem of a savage future in which we discover ourselves to be cartoon consumers locked into a sanitary totalitarian plastic tapeloop, our every move monitored, our every impulse predetermined by the invisible spider god. The picture is familiar. From within the field of science fiction, writers like Frederik Pohl have been touching on the vision for decades now. Post-Hollywood movies like *Westworld* or *The Stepford Wives* have vulgarized some of the more obvious implications of treating robots and humans as being nightmarishly interchangeable. The significant fact about Disneyland is that it incarnates all the surreal meaningfulness of film itself; it embodies the *meaning* of all these echoes and prefigurations with a compelling hypnotic clarity that burns through the fabric of most fictional attempts at satirizing it. (We're addressing here a difficulty that confronts all satirists of the extremes of American life — so movie-like in its self-presentation [cf. Erving Goffman's *The Presentation of Self in Everyday Life (1959) 1986*] — hence the length of this prologue.) The idea of Disneyland is too exhaustively present in the fact of Disneyland for most satire to be anything more than a kind of after-the-fact nagging. Anything said about Disneyland is inherently *belated.* Whatever you do so, Walt already meant it.

So it takes a brave and formidable writer to tackle his vision successfully, this meaning system too hot and dense for casual use, even if you don't name it, as Kit Reed very carefully doesn't in *Magic Time* (Putnam, 1980), which is set in a near future America strikingly like the America of today, except for holofilms, a few stray gimmicks, and the presence of Happy Habitat, "a unique blend of Disneyland and Fantasy Island," as the jacket copy puts it, blowing her cover right off and arousing dangerously high expectations in the reader, though there are some signs that Ms Reed is fully aware of the nature of the task she has set out for herself. For instance, she has presented the first-person narratives of her four protagonists as a kind of tape transcription, a script perhaps for a holofilm of the mind mirroring the filmic origins of the world she is attempting to describe, which does point in the direction of a confrontation with her material. Bits of narrative her protagonists cannot tell themselves are even labelled "outtakes," as though the reader had VIP privileges in the cutting room; and their adventures in trying to escape from Happy Habitat are constantly tracked by cameras, harangued by voiceovers, hyped by trailers which they themselves can watch on the omnipresent television screens. All well and good, you'd think; Ms Reed is showing commendable task consciousness. But unfortunately, from beginning to end, the actual tone of the telling of *Magic Time*, in whoever's voice, is so amiable as to seem pixillated, and nothing could be more fatal than whimsy in a book the very mention of whose subject matter — as I've been arguing — burns right through mere fictional wordplay. So *Magic Time* ends up being something rather unusual, a likeable book that gets the back up, because there's something unnatural — something monstrous — in a tale so virginal in its telling, so prepubescent in its clean clear tone, and so ominously and obscenely pregnant with meaning.

The story is swift, nor do the four protagonists much complicate matters with their varying points of view. Tame holofilm maker Boone Castle finds himself trapped in Happy Habitat as a live exhibit in a continuing drama starring five kidnapped people. Elderly Eveline is trapped in the Golden Acres section of the park, a senior citizen's village where she is encouraged in her intense cosmetic battle against aging, but solely so that she can be used as an unwitting bit player in one of the front-stage Habitat melodramas until she bites the dust. Kaa Naaji, Indian inventor of a method of extracting energy from cow dung, has come voluntarily to Happy Habitat, where he hopes to recover for himself a sense of springtide adventure, but soon falls in love with big tough violent Luce, a woman guard disgusted by him and infatuated with Boone Castle. In one way or another, these four gradually discover what the reader — being versed in the meaning of Disneyland — has known from the first: that Happy Habitat is a totalitarian control fantasy; that staff, customers and prisoners are all victims together under the skin, and are subject to manipulation and interchange, like robots. After ganging up together, the four star escapers — for the management treats their battle to get out as another part of the ongoing show — finally penetrate to the inner sanctum, a Disney-like cottage in a fake meadow, where they confront Pa, the owner of Happy Habitat. Unsurprisingly, given some of the sick jokes still floating about to the effect that Walt Disney was cryogenically frozen upon his death in 1966 and will one day rise to save us all like King Arthur, Pa turns out to be a wired-up brain-in-a-box, having defeated death in this fashion. At some length, very obligingly, Pa now expounds upon his philosophy:

> . . . you have seen how harmonious I have made everything. Rather than re-create nature here, I have chosen to improve on it — the gardens, the functional objects, the avenues were all conceived to be more beautiful than anything in nature, more disciplined, and that is all part of the plan.

And so forth. The plan is simple: Pa intends to sanitize the rest of America by force. He is of course thwarted, but only — we are intended to understand — after a fashion, because when Boone Castle gets out of the park at long last, he finds that he has by no means defeated the Happy Habitat system of meaning, for he has become a star. Perhaps *Magic Time* is supposed to be the book of the movie. Witty; but wit is not enough. There is no way grace-notes can contain the pregnancy of the dream of America Ms Reed has elected to score for virginal. The monster is not laid, merely tickled a little.

A couple of minor books here, though one of them is very thick. Victoria Schochet and John Silbersack of Berkley Publishing Corporation have put together in *The Berkley Showcase Volume 1: New Writings in Science Fiction and Fantasy* (Berkley, 1980) what they have managed to describe as "a nonprofit-oriented house anthology," by which they presumably intend to say that making a profit was not their prime objective, though what they *do* say is that *not* making a profit was their prime objective, which is not the same thing at all. One hopes they're still employed. The anthology itself is a very mixed bag. "The Princess and the Bear" by Orson Scott Card, though wrapped in cellophane, is still a very neat and rather moving fable about the nature of sexual love, among other things. "Sergeant Pepper" by Karl Hansen, though I wouldn't much care to unpack its moral implications a decade after Viet Nam, mixes medicine and warfare at a high old kinetic pitch. "Billy Big-Eyes" by Howard Waldrop, with far more detail than content, deals rather weepily with tragic love in a universe where Space Scouts have eyes surgically modified the better to read stars by; perhaps a series is in the offing. The remainder — unfortunately including a routine exercise in feminism from Elizabeth A Lynn, and a totally opaque tale by Janet E Morris about (I think) alchemy at the time (maybe) of Paracelsus — might be from some creative writing workshop, I mean the stories that *didn't* get read.

Lee Killough has written a couple of decent novels, and some good short stories, a few of the latter being published in this magazine. Because there is nothing precisely offensive about *The Monitor, The Miners and the Shree* (Del Rey, 1980), perhaps it should be passed over in silence, after a minute or two. The Shree are an avian species. The miners have been mining the Shree planet illegally for hundreds of years. The stiff-necked Monitor and her chums make an official visit to the planet, but before they can find out anything of interest are cast into the wilderness (by the miners) and rescued (by the Shree). For 150 pages, we follow the Monitor's gradual cottoning on to the benefits which the miners have bestowed upon the proud, twittering Shree. At the end of the book, she defends the miners at the galactic trial. Almost all of the text is padding, and the story was probably originally conceived as a juvenile. There are few threatening words, and not an original one. What can you say?

Now for the thick one. *Shiva Descending* (Avon, 1980), by Gregory Benford (who should know better but has maybe been hoodwinked by the Protestant work ethic) and William Rotsler (who *did* write *Zandra*), is probably not the worst novel written about a huge meteor on a collision course with our planet, but then who's keeping score? Will Shiva semi-total Terra? Will the President go bonkers from too much strain and too much sex with his secretary? Will the nutcase astronaut go finally around the bend as well? These questions, and many many more, receive answers. It all takes 400 pages. NASA gets into the act, Russia intervenes, pro-Shiva sects develop, and the whole fabric of civilization begins to shred. Shiva is eventually diverted, shifted into orbit, slated to become a space station: ending all these woes. Of main interest, at least to readers of Benford's other books, may be the way in which the bureaucratic corruption of NASA and of government in general can be read pretty explicitly as a description of the entropic loss of vigor of Western civilization itself as the century passes on beyond the Moon landing. Though ostensibly a tale of human valor and technological triumph against almost insuperable odds, beneath all the acres of blockbuster filibustering there is a fin-de-siècle melancholy to the book, telling us that not all is well, and even suggesting a few reasons for our sense of unease. It's some compensation for all the nonsense on top.

The case of Barry N Malzberg becomes yet more complex with the publication of a new collection of short fiction, by no means all of it sf or fantasy, though Doubleday continues to market him as a genre product. *The Man Who Loved the Midnight Lady* (Doubleday, 1980), which assembles stories written for the most part over the past half decade, further deepens the sense of perplexity, of alarmed alienated implication, one feels on entering his calcined solipsistic universe. Once again, these stories present a world whose colors have been ashed down into a desolate, grey, weirdly primitive tonal inscape dominated, at least in the stories he himself seems to consider his finest work, by that dense monomaniacal single voice with which his readers have become painfully familiar over the past decade or so; which is thoroughly to their advantage, because it is a powerful tool. Always it is the same voice, grey, flat, intense, obsessive, unstoppable, almost always couched in the claustrophobic narrative-present tense, and seemingly humorless. But here's a rub. As he makes clear in the remarkably modest, revealing and intelligent commentary he has supplied for this publication, Malzberg thinks that he is at times a *funny* writer. *Malzberg?* There is a shock of revelation in this, and maybe it's not entirely the reader's fault if the element of hilarity in many Malzberg tales tends to escape him (see below). I personally once had the same incapacity — to register humorousness — with another, very different American writer. William Faulkner. Because of the deadpan ferocity, the claustrophobic *closeness* of his manner of telling his horrific tall tales, because I could not escape his unblinking eye, I could not get the distance to register the appalling hilarity of what he was saying, until (on some collegiate occasion) I was told he was funny, and suddenly realized I had been blind to it. If he shares nothing else with Faulkner (and I rather suspect he's closer to Faulkner than to some of the writers he homages in this volume, like Damon Runyon), Malzberg does certainly share that claustrophobically unblinking eye, and I did find his claim to be funny to work as a releaser in the same way. Because the eye winked! That loony urban driving trapped voice *knows itself!*

All the same, when the voice comes at us in all its purity — solipsistic, perspectiveless, tortured, self-mutilated, as in stories like "Here, for Just a While," or "In the Stocks" — then it's not at all surprising that one tends to miss gradations in the tone, a twitch of the eyebrow. Though he's certainly at his most intense in stories like these, it could be argued that Malzberg comes closer to genuine mastery in stories written more or less to order, like "Indigestion," or the non-sf or -fantasy tales he published in *Alfred Hitchcock's Mystery Magazine*, like "Varieties of Religious Experience," or the superb collaborations with Bill Pronzini, the best of which is probably "Another Burnt-Out Case"; it is also very hilarious.

There is also the sense that *The Man Who Loved the Midnight Lady* is a transitional collection, and that Malzberg, after dozens of books, may only now be coming into full control of his complete range. Certainly the sharp density of many of these stories strikes a note of relief and anticipation, especially after some of the tired novels of the mid 70s. It feels good to be able to hope [and eventually to be able to read a novel as mature and rounded and at points hilarious as *The Remaking of Sigmund Freud* (1985) *1986*].

The Magazine of Fantasy and Science Fiction//December 1980

10//FSF9//Goldin/Yermakov/Preuss/Adams/Card

By 1970 it was no longer possible. Suddenly there was too much to read. Before that point, somewhere in the United States of America, someone or other was managing to keep up with everything everyone was publishing in science fiction or fantasy, and the knowledge that he or she (probably he back then) was out there keeping an eagle eye on all the big names and all the strays was oddly reassuring to at least some of the rest of us, because we knew that a genre small enough to read was a genre small enough to understand. Somehow you couldn't be snuck up on from behind.

Now there's no one to defend our rear. A genre too big is a genre you can't see the boundaries of. [I was thinking here of Erving Goffman's definition of the legible world of "fatefulness" as involving "a play of events that can be initiated and realized in a space and time small enough to be fully witnessed." There's some further play with this concept in the essay on James Blish, "Scholia, Seasoned with Crabs, Blish Is," collected below as Chapter 13 *1986*.] As readers and writers and editors and reviewers we become at last classic victims of the dehumanizing scale of the Twentieth Century. Ultimately there's no *we* left at all. And in the new environment of media packaging that treats fans as *consumers* (another Twentieth Century process we seemed immune from, maybe because we were once very small), it's become increasingly difficult to get the feel of new books, which more and more take on the aspect of products assembled for consumption. What certainly sounds original and from-the-heart in the first novel of (say) Nicholas Yermakov, author of several urgent, hilarious, astringent stories for this magazine, may or may not turn out all but indistinguishable from other products put together to fill the space-opera marketing slot. Orson Scott Card may be exploring harsh catechisms of private pain, or maybe he's a merchant. Who knows? Who can tell the dark night of the soul from dark-night-of-the-soul style? And who is Stephen Goldin when he's not a Doc Smith plant?

Stephen Goldin can (at least minimally) be described as the author of *A World Called Solitude*, which he dedicates to his wife, so that he may actually mean it all, and which reads rather like late-early-middle Robert Silverberg stuck in molasses. Though by no means sharp-witted, *A World Called Solitude* (Doubleday, 1981) earnestly and at times charmingly combines Silverbergian Weltschmerz (a neurotic/solitary/urban scientist — who has invented faster-than-light travel and been framed by his government while at the same time failing his wife sexually and in other ways — escapes crashed prison spaceship, sets up life alone and morosely self-pitying on a deserted planet chock-a-block with relics of magical technology) and Doc Smith epic (years after the above, a nubile girl soldier also crashes on the same planet while fleeing vile aliens making undeclared war on human space and tries to shake hero out of Silverbergian fugue so he can save humanity for the second time running), but never cashes in on the ironies churned up in this melange. When Birk the anti-hero responds to the warrior lady's prodding by telling her he's still afraid of being treated as a criminal back on Earth, she ripostes with the unanswerably deranged estimate that he should expect the politicians to forgive him for being Gilgamesh and Christ in one package *on their turf*. When the bemused neurotic Birk quizzes her Howzat? she tells him howzat:

> Just look at it. The Commonwealth is at war with these aliens. You captured one of their officers alive. You invented a machine that jams their ships. You discovered an entire planet filled with exotic weapons and new technology. I don't think any single person could make a bigger contribution to the war effort.

All this plus inventing FTL travel. *While severely depressed.* Birk had never added it all up before, and is now convinced that the warrior lass is right, the entire galaxy *needs* him, and the politicos back home are gonna be *grateful*. The rest of us, who had given this scenario the respect it deserved some time previously, like maybe on page three, may be excused from wondering whether *A World Called Solitude* is an honest though slightly dumb novel about the salvation in human terms of a hyperventilating Silverbergian soul far from Manhattan, or perhaps just *Fantasy Island.* Take your pick. If I had to, I'd plump for sincerity, slightly stewed.

Now about Nicholas Yermakov. *Journey from Flesh* (Berkley Books, 1981) gives off a competent post-Delany tang in its opening scenes, which (after a teaser prologue) establish paramed-rated phase-shift navigator Alan Dreyfus having a spree in Port City on a blah planet where he meets a pack of 1960s-style "bohemians" in a bar, along with a mercenary once in the service of the dread musclebound Shahin but now seemingly addicted to a vampire lizard whose bite seems to grant him paranormal empathy to such a degree that he can (or maybe it's the lizard who can) *tell the truth* about anyone down to the last soul-baring detail, for a fee. Thinking it's a scam, Dreyfus dares him to go ahead, at which point (we have reached page 11) Nicholas Yermakov came to what I'd guess was a crisis decision nexus. Should he take on the task of actually presenting some of the truths Dreyfus is going to be saddled with, thus making some novelistic attempt at rendering *something* of the baroque inscapes of the human enterprise centuries hence and light-years gone, or should he just stop giving us hints that he's writing an actual novel and get on with the *job.* Read on:

> A brutal encounter. Alan Dreyfus stripped and flayed. John [the mercenary] laughed, he smiled, he charmed and told me things about myself that were so deeply buried that my conscious mind had never thought to resurrect them.

End of novel. Beginning of job. After this shameless flapdoodle we learn absolutely nothing about Dreyfus of any interest beyond what Doc Smith could have told anyone in his sleep. What remains is space opera, subtly dishonoured by pretense. The lizards are (of course) a valiant dying species from Viet-Nam-like Xerxes Something Or Other exploited by the arrogant and merciless Shahin for the juice or something that turns men into heldentenors I mean Shahin; once himself bitten by a lizard, Dreyfus begins to see the light and, helped by the Navy and the "bohemians" and Viet-Nam-sergeant-like Creed Steiger, he saves Xerxes, though only with the *additional* help of — but that would give the story away. It's all rather a shame. With his title taken from a poem by Theodore Roethke, with his dedication made not only to personal friends but to public friends Norman Spinrad *and* Harlan Ellison as well, with long extracts from Coleridge's *Rime of the Ancient Mariner* acutely uncomfortable in their new setting, and with a numbing Afterword in which the author tells us carefully (in better prose than his novel) how the book I think he never wrote got thought up (but not how he never wrote it), a good writer thoroughly adrift has betrayed both himself and the beginnings of some good ideas; he is visibly the wrong emcee for this potted package tour of the space opera market.

Paul Preuss may or may not have less talent than Nicholas Yermakov, but does fit himself with pleasing and appropriate anonymity into the job of telling his polished barmy traditional tale of time and space travel, which ends (as usual) in Gordian knots *I* had no sword for. Like all true hard sf, *Re-entry* (Bantam Books, 1981) is a novel which is what it means to be — glossy, technophilic, ornate, savvy about the frontiers of knowledge, power-obsessed in the name of hardnosed realism: great on carapace; vacuous on the inner depths. But cyborg-android computer-assisted telepathic confabs and the kinetic interaction between Man and bronco black holes aside, the main thing about a hard sf novel is that, whatever it's about, it doesn't take the micky out of it. True to form, *Re-entry* copes unsmilingly with a tale too convoluted to more than hint at. A man wishes to change his lifestyle by going back in time through a black hole in a spaceship and tutoring himself on a primitive planet rather like Australia, and does. The oldest wisest woman in the universe has a watching brief and lends a helping hand (it gets complicated here). A corrupt dictator is tied into pretzels (or isn't). A planet-wide experiment in evolution is seriously toxified by all of the above. There are spaceships out of *Star Wars* and characters whose actions have a high albedo but whose hearts are illegible (or empty) as the space between the stars in Hollywood. It's all a lot of fun. Brand merchandise. Which means that you do get what you pay for.

I don't think anyone could pretend that Douglas Adams' *The Hitchhiker's Guide to the Galaxy* (Harmony Books, 1980 [previous UK publication 1979]), which novelizes part of his extraordinarily successful BBC radio series of the same name, ever amounted to much more than a job of media transplant for its author, who, having once already told the jokes and the story they engendered, was, very likely, at the point he wrote the novel, also preparing to run the whole package through yet another transformation — into a television series, also successful. But whatever form this blatant package comes in, it's a joy.

To begin with, *Hitchhiker* is indeed a novel about how to travel free around the galaxy; somewhere in between it is a cosmological fable about the construction of our Earth as a gigantic living computer designed to solve the riddle of existence (all costs covered by the creatures who had us built and who manifest themselves in the shape of white mice so they can watch us experiment); but it all ends before anything is properly resolved because there is a sequel, *The Restaurant at the End of the Universe*, episodes of which appear earlier in the radio and tv versions than they do in print, which is sometimes confusing. But no thumb-waving at the actual flow of the story can do much more than deflate the underlying jokes which clearly structure the sometimes slightly pixy moves of the tale. If we hear that Earth is about to be demolished to make way for an interstellar turnpike, then sooner or later Earth *will* be demolished, and all her citizenry die, with the exception of some white mice — and the heroes, who are hitchhiking at the time. Significantly, Adams did some script work for *Monty Python's Flying Circus*, the famous 1960s British tv revue, where similar deadpan leaps shaped many of the best sketches.

Given its music-hall premises, it's no surprise that the tone of *Hitchhiker* is sometimes damagingly sophomoric, that there is a recurring taint of collegiate wit in the naming of silly names and the descriptions of silly alcoholic beverages; and the smooth finger-licking cynicism of the book does sometimes remind one of Kurt Vonnegut's lesser moments. But so it goes. There is enough joy throughout, enough tooth to the zaniness, and enough rude knowingness about media-hype versions of science fiction, to make *Hitchhiker* one of the genre's rare genuinely funny books.

We come to a star writer of the new age when stranger beds with stranger. We do not know whether to laugh or cry. Neither does Orson Scott Card, maybe. At the heart of all his work to date a compulsive cold technical polish unflaggingly exposes to view some of the oddest mortal coils the genre has yet presented to its readership, but I for one have never been able to tell if the innards he formaldehydes are gut or plasteel. This drive of his to the interior nerve — which sometimes reads like a grenade held to the stomach — *seems* to sound authentic all right, but only sometimes; there is a pervading lack of gearedness between text and reader, which may in part be due to problems of focus engendered by that expanded commercialized horizonless genre we've been moaning about for the last couple thousand words.

It's certainly the case that Card's effect, when tested by comparison with earlier writers in the genre, can seem mannered, decadent, *villainous*; and he can read like a professional spelunker only pretending to take risks in the blood caverns of the invaded heart. This is clearest in some of the stories in *Unaccompanied Sonata and Other Stories* (Dial Press, 1981) which are old genre fancies reclothed; "Mortal Gods," for instance, takes the idea that there is an elevated poignance in being human and mortal in a universe of longlifers for whom death is a mystery and who worship our transience, and so over-deftly manipulates the pathos of the tale that the reader tends to finish the story feeling rather like Queen for a Day: consumed. So that reader may well feel a certain suspicion, and, on coming across more original-seeming work, may feel once-bitten about following Card's lead into the theme-park Deep. Take "Kingsmeat," which reads like a toboggan ride downwards into late Twentieth Century paradigm country, where the knives are out. On a conquered human colony planet, anthropophagous alien rulers in a magic castle demand living flesh of their victims; to do their bidding (lest more terrible diktats emerge), a human Shepherd periodically strides through the Disney village full of captives, selecting limbs and breasts and organs for the aliens' repast, meanwhile calming the donors with his magic wand. Suddenly the planet is liberated, and he is put on trial. Though the colonists come to recognize that he has been playing Shepherd to prevent a massacre of all human stock, they refuse to let him go free; if he has played God, then like so many gods he must be put in bondage and gradually eviscerated, though kept alive to watch his people smile. So. Does the story work as allegory, as a kind of dream of Duty that General Douglas MacArthur might have had in 1951, or does it evoke more powerfully that abyssal pornotopic cruelty endemic to much of the art of today (for we are in a time of troubles) and whose roots (one supposes) are in texts like *Story of O*? Other stories in the book, like the well-known "Ender's Game" and "Unaccompanied Sonata" itself, likewise chill the mind until it is too numb for catharsis. In the end, glitter blinds, and Card abandons us there, in the dark.

[This column finished off with a review of Gene Wolfe's *Gene Wolfe's Book of Days*, but it seemed better to stick those paragraphs into the sequence of Wolfe reviews in Chapter 18, which see.]

The Magazine of Fantasy and Science Fiction//February 1982

11//FSF10//Reaves/Sheffield/Young/Griffin/Kingsbury

Here are five books. They come from four different publishers, and are all paperback originals. One of them is fairly but not insultingly bad, one is competent but cursory, one is cursory but winded, one is long and intense but lacks either blind men or an elephant, and one is very long and exuberant and if it had any blind men in it its protagonists would eat them. These books have been ranked and will be reviewed in ascending order of ambition, which (unusually) is almost the same as their order of merit (according to me). At a time when all too many ersatz visions (or *treatments*) reach the marketplace positively dropsical with hype, it is worth noting that none of the five books under review is unduly bloated. Indeed, the only real failure of means to end — Robert F Young's *The Last Yggdrasil* — is a failure of excessive modesty.

We can start with J Michael Reaves's dim but decent *Darkworld Detective* (Bantam Books, 1982), a pottering assemblage of four linked stories. The Darkworld of the title is called Ja-Lur, and the shamus is called Kamus. Ja-Lur is a Darkworld because its sun is so dim it even seems dim to its native inhabitants [implying a Platonic standard of ideal right brightness which, one suspects, J Michael Reaves did not consciously long to evoke *1986*], *and* because the Darklord, whose domain is controlled through magic, grimly dominates the even darker dark side of Darkworld. I have no idea why the shamus is called Kamus. Kamus the shamus stars in each of the stories, narrating each of them in a style about as close to Raymond Chandler as Kai Lung gets to Confucius. And though each story takes its title, ostensibly with some reason, from a different famous Terran novel — two American private eye thrillers, one classic English detective novel, and the worst of the James Bonds — Kamus the shamus narrates each of them in exactly the same tone of voice, which, as the stories unremittingly resemble one another in almost every particular, may be fair enough, but which does rather beg the question of the nature of the homage being offered.

But this may be too harsh. Failed or nonexistent homage aside, what remains is mostly straightforward fun. As the book progresses, the shamus (a gumshoe) finds himself, because of his half-Dark blood and his far from inconspicuous position as the only detective on the planet, becoming more and more deeply involved in a Jai-Lur-wide conflict between the forces of science fiction and the forces of heroic fantasy. The modus vivendi between the Darklord's fantasy domain and the Galactic Unity's high-tech interstellar imperium is beginning to unravel as Shadownight approaches. Mysterious figures start trying to hire young Kamus. Mysterious assaults are mysteriously survived by the brave young detective, who is increasingly haunted by the mystery of the identity of his father, a mysterious figure of a father from the Dark Lands who raped Kamus's mother-to-be and split. Mysterious omens point the canny shamus in the direction of the Darklord, who resides in the Dark Spire. I guess, he thinks, it was inevitable. And off he treks therefore into the Dark, dogged by whores, demons, ambitious women, bad beer, debutantes, lousy spells, walking skeletons, gods, dwarves, giants, androids, millionaires, traitors, troubadours and bureaucrats, but nothing out of the ordinary; there in the Dark, in the caverns of the Dark not-unphallic Spire, Kamus (for it is he) duly works out his destiny, identifies his Dad (one guess who), stitches the world back together again, and closes off his tale by quoting the last lines of *Casablanca*.

What is there to complain about?

Far more energetic, and somewhat more culpable in its partial failure to deliver the goods, is Charles Sheffield's *My Brother's Keeper* (Ace Books, 1982). It's a very odd novel indeed. Starting off with some intensity to explore a split-brain problem to end all split-brain problems, it soon drops the issue like a couple of hot potatoes untimely ripped, and sidesteps into a Laumeresque international chase thriller in which the guy(s) with the split brain hurtle(s) around the world in search of a MacGuffin totally unrelated to his (their) intriguing dilemma.

What happens at the beginning of the novel is elaborately improbable but absolutely necessary if there's going to be a story at all. Pianist Lionel Salkind is contacted by Leo Foss, his identical twin, who is in some kind of deep trouble — which soon comes home to roost when the brothers' helicopter is sabotaged and crashes, horribly wounding both of them. Lionel (who tells the tale) awakens in the hospital to discover that in the crash he has lost the right hemisphere of his brain, along with some other organs and little bits, but that brother Leo has not only lost the *left* hemisphere of *his* brain but almost everything else as well. What detritus of Leo remains is legally dead. But a brilliant bad-tempered brain surgeon, as the pianist-narrator soon discovers, has planted the right hemisphere of Leo's brain like a hot potato into the vacancy in Lionel's own damaged skull, and Lionel has become his brother's keeper. Now it may be the case that the left hemisphere of the brain governs self-awareness as well as speech, but from his right-hand fastness Leo soon starts homing in on Lionel like Palmer Eldritch, and it begins to look as though we're in for a pretty complex — and maybe pretty gripping — examination of anything and everything from mind/brain conundrums to the question of the real location of the identity function or soul, from doppelgangers through secret sharers through puppet masters, right on down to knock-knock jokes.

But it turns out that Sheffield has no intention of juggling these potatoes for more than a few pages. And what Charles Sheffield doesn't intend to do, Charles Sheffield doesn't do; he is a writer of considerable force and knowing clarity, even when he's playing hooky. With devastating speed, Lionel adjusts to the loss of half his brain and the gain of half a kibitzer, screws his nurse, gets kidnapped by the singularly incompetent hoods who are after the MacGuffin Leo seemingly stashed away somewhere, escapes from their clutches, dashes to India, gets re-captured, re-escapes, dashes to Arabia, traps a sadistic female villain in a zoo with hundreds of poisonous snakes, and finds the MacGuffin. And at every chance he/they/it get(s), Leo's right hemisphere plays knock-knock games with Lionel's left, augments his brother's powers whenever necessary, and seems thoroughly to enjoy the ride. As we all do. We are carried along. But there is a point (it is a point when we are dumped off the last page) that some more serious questions come up. Will the Six Million Dollar Piano Man, for instance, given the fact that musical ability is centered in the right hemisphere and Leo probably thinks Milhaud's a ski resort, ever tickle the keys with feeling again? Will Lionel find happiness in the four arms of the two girls enamoured of one(?) guy, or will Leo start sticking his oar in? (Does Leo *have* an oar? On a condo basis maybe?) As surely as there will [should *1986*] be further installments to this caper of the brother's keeper, just as surely Sheffield is going to have to begin to think about the issues he's left behind.

It's rather a shame about *The Last Yggdrasil* (Del Rey, 1982), Robert F Young's overstretched novella in which humanity spreads to the victim stars, continuing to commit ecocide all the while. To begin with the title itself, there is something at the heart of the concept of the Norse World-Tree that deeply precludes the notion of there being *more than one* of them. In any case, the underlying ecological puzzle is too transparently simple to fool even a farmer, even a *human* farmer, even a human agrobusiness monocrop planetary-suicide-for-profit farmer. The Yggdrasil in question is the last of a species of apparently semi-sentient dryad-souled trees that have colonized the vast plains of Genji 5. Arriving much later on the scene, when only one huge tree remains to overshadow the mysteriously organic aboriginal village it dominates, human colonists soon hire an "interstellar tree removal service" to get rid of what they consider an unsightly monster. But even the most careless reader will have noted that the terribly valuable crop which the colonists harvest *only* grows in proximity to this one remaining tree, and will not be surprised with the revelation at story's close that this last Yggdrasil nestled at the heart of a complex ecology — even the village turns out to be part of its root system — and that its destruction signals the end of profit-taking for the farmers.

Though eked out to barely book length by undue repetition of themes and omens we have already memorized, the story itself is strangely moving. The progressive murder of the tree, branch by branch, makes for genuinely painful reading. The owner and employees of TreeCo are all walking wounded; the desert they are hired to make out of a living world is convincingly analogued to the twisted poverty of their hearts. The central character, who is involved (unsurprisingly in a Young story) in the long devastation of unhappy sexual passion, finds himself haunted by the dryad of the great tree (whom the Del Rey artist renders as a dyspeptic Tinkerbell) but continues to dismember the leaf and bole which were her garment, partly to exorcise despair over his human woman, a holovision reporter who sleeps with sexy men whenever she has a mind to; the sense that to be a failed human is to contaminate the world pervades the text with resigned melancholy. Shorter, *The Last Yggdrasil* could have been a fable of some strength. Longer, with enough room to portray a rational farming community (however unrealistic that might seem) and a genuine conflict between Progress and Life, we might have been gifted with a powerful novel about our state.

Precisely why Russell M Griffin's hideous and hilarious third novel, *The Blind Men and the Elephant* (Timescape/Pocket Books, 1982), benefits so much from being read as science fiction it may be of some interest to try to work out. As sf, it is certainly marginal. The action, which is tangled and mundane and permits no heroes, takes place in our own latter days in the urban backwaters of a Massachusetts abandoned by the century and depicted by Griffin with the intense clammy obsessive surplusage of detail-work that is a first sign of creative love/hate. Like John Sladek, some of whose techniques and concerns he shares in this novel, Griffin exhibits all the buttonholing relentlessness of the born exile in his street-wise scrying of the alien habitat which immures him. The result is some remarkable snapshots of contemporary America.

But unlike Sladek, Griffin stops short of any attempt to render the world we live in as being not only foolish and cruel, but also unhinged at root. Absurd. Void of meaning. Too often in *Blind Men* sarcasm or a slightly creepy indignation tend to substitute for anything like a full depiction of the horrors Griffin — if his plot is any evidence — seems very clearly to want to grapple with. It is here, however, that the science fiction element in the book transforms missed opportunities into at least partial success, mundane sarcasms into fable.

Incompetent weatherman for a decrepit Mafia-linked local television station, for which he also serves as the rear end of a childrens'-hour horse, Burton Lessingwell thinks he may have struck it rich when he finds himself in control of a monstrous freak nicknamed the Elephant Man, presumably because of his resemblance to the real-life nineteenth-century English freak. But whatever's wrong with Macduff, the current Elephant Man, it's nothing so mundane as a mere sclerosis of nerve padding or whatever. Macduff is very weird, constantly in pain, and obscenely acute, though he can only remember flashes of what seems to be an impossibly brief life. These flashes of memory usually recall bits of his time at a Catholic boarding school whose corridors are crammed (a la Sladek) with venal and/or fetish-ridden priests. Indeed, his whole circumambient world — just like Roderick's in Sladek's *Roderick* — is suffused with avarice, though here in backwater Massachusetts it's generally *failed* avarice. Burton Lessingwell certainly doesn't care much about Macduff's pain or his cruel narrow past, visualizing him as a human interest spectacle rather than as a person; soon enough, though, he's forced to sharpen his attention when he notices that he and Macduff are constantly being shadowed, day and night, by identical men in sunglasses, the Blind Men of the title.

From this point the plot darkens, in fact plunges sickeningly into a science-fiction explanation of how Macduff was manufactured about five years earlier *in vitro* out of (I think; I always bugger this sort of thing up) cancer cells extracted from a male gonad. But however it is put, it's clear that Macduff is nothing but a great bloated cancer; the ultimate homunculus; a walking contagion. And this last may literally be the case. The Blind Men — as in *The President's Analyst* from 1967 they are government agents — have been trying to trace Macduff after his escape from the lab and his disappearance from places like the school for orphans he had secretly attended, precisely because he may be contagious as well as embarrassing. He may — or may not, for the novel ends before we can be told — be about to infect all of humanity with homuncular cancer (which tends to attack the skin or crust), in the same way that humanity has spread its contaminating urban detritus across the globe, Yggdrasil beware.

Or that's how I read the message behind Griffin's insertion of so maculate a conception into the dying world of Butler, Massachusetts, though it's hard to know for sure, because the text ends before its implications have a chance to settle down. And I'm afraid that, without the apertures a science-fictional reading opens, the creation of Macduff might seem a particularly tasteless sample of Grand Guignol at its sensation-mongering worst. A science-fictional reading of Macduff opens his savaged state to all the cognitive exculpations that the genre can claim, sometimes with justice, to have a lien on. For genre readers, Macduff, presented in his anguish and terrible solitude and loathsomeness, may seem no less than an imago of the Whole Man to come; Macduff may *spawn*; Macduff may establish paranormal empathy with the birds and beasts and lead them out of Hamelin; Macduff may be rescued by a wise man in a toga from the far future; Macduff may in truth be an alien tyke whose parents are beaming in right now; or as an Immaterial Sentience Macduff may whisk *himself* off to the stars like a James Tiptree possum. Who knows?

All that we can say is that this exculpatory work is done for Griffin by the conventions he has evoked, and that it allows us to stomach the horrors and relish the hilarities of his text. All the same, there is a troubling vacancy at the heart of the book. We are more or less told that Macduff has begun life as a tabula rasa — blanker even than the infant robot in *Roderick*, that book this book so much brings to mind — and that he has had to assemble a human nature for himself. It does strike one that if this long problematic task of becoming human had comprised the hard knotted gravamen of *The Blind Men and the Elephant*, it might have been able to deal squarely, without resting on exculpations to sanitize the text, with its nightmarish hero. It might have been a novel that stretched and tested — instead of hiding within — the boundaries of the genre. It's not enough to learn in passing that Macduff watches daytime television avariciously, and that he creates language and analyzes human behavior out of his experience of quiz games and soap operas, for that doesn't amount to much more than an old joke about American life, and no longer a very good one. There is a paucity here. Some central questions are being begged. What was potentially a large-minded black book of the soul turns out to be a jape. Hilarious certainly; but vacant, too.

Let us clear the air a little and finish off with a vibrant good-tempered saga about cannibalism and group marriages and war and great-hearted death rituals and family-dominated politics and explosive cultural breakthroughs, all played out against the harsh tapestries of a world not entirely unlike *Dune*'s but inhabited in this case by human types so drastically estranged from their off-planet origins that they think of the orbiting generation-starship that had dumped them here as God. They can know no better. But it is a sign of the muscular optimism of Donald Kingsbury's *Courtship Rite* (Timescape/Simon and Schuster, 1982) — and of the enormous rewards he confers on those who are most successful in actually operating the world he has created — that this worship of a high-albedo God scooting across heaven reads not as superstitious but as highly pragmatic: God clearly exists, so you might as well believe in Him/Her; and to those who help themselves by believing, God has clearly in the past provided all sorts of highly remunerative Promethean hints and tidbits, for the tablets that fall like manna out of the sky are in fact memory chips, nor is there any sign that the largesse is about to cease. Sequels are promised.

So what Kingsbury has given us is a success story. Against the radical scarcity and general precariousness of life in the alien ecosystem of the planet Geta, his human outcasts have cobbled together for themselves a most remarkable culture. Cannibalism lies at the heart of the evolution of Getan life; it controls population growth, punishes the wicked by feeding the good, weeds out the unfit in childhood (though the reader may feel a bit queasy at how effortlessly Getans manage to define moral and other fitnesses in terms of their offsprings' luck at surviving highly competitive agonistic ordeals), controls warfare through the taboo against killing more than you can eat, and shapes individual lives into a sociobiologist's dream of altruism, for old Getans positively (though one must suppose vicariously) *relish* the thought of being incorporated into the young of their clan. And human skin makes good hides, too. But much of the pleasure of the text lies in the gradual accumulation of significant detail designed to show how cannibalism and genetical expertise (the word for *priest* is *biologist*) and group marriages and clan-loyalties all intersect in a triumphant adaptive response to hardship.

The story that gives the book its title also works to demonstrate the triumph of the fittest. Already high in the councils of the ambitious and increasingly dominant Kaiel clan, a five-marriage (three brothers and two unrelated women) is told it cannot wed the brilliant scientist of its collective choice, but must instead, for reasons of Realpolitik, court a total stranger. She turns out to be a heretical pacifist of great influence in an area the Kaiel are eager to dominate. The courtship turns out to be arduous, but the prize is power and glory and magnificent love-making and not being lunch. In order to assess her worthiness as a wife (and to keep the plot boiling for hundreds of pages), the most valour-obsessed of the brothers imposes a seven-step Trial of Death on the pacifist lady, which — need it be said — she eventually and triumphantly survives. And the other clans are defeated. And the small chips fall from heaven. And the brilliant scientist begins to transform the whole planet. And the five-marriage gets to wed *her*, too.

This may seem cornball, but it's exhilarating to read. The only cornball element that fails to persuade is a most implausible spy/courtesan/clone, trusted member of the spy/courtesan/clone clan, who screws all of the brothers in different disguises and generally manipulates everyone from behind a plethora of arrases. Though she's an attractive enough creation, her presence is a gimmicky distraction in a novel that is patently meant not only to entertain but also to make the reader think.

Of course even the best Libertarian science fiction scenarios are irremediably rigged, and in any case I'm by no means clear that Kingsbury would call himself a Libertarian, though it's certainly true that as a metaphor for self-help and Social Darwinism in general cannibalism *does* have something of a non-Welfare-State ring to it. Perhaps, in the end, it's impossible to dramatize an argument in a work of fiction without rigging the outcome; fiction is precisely rigging. When ideologues write fiction, however, they tend to claim to be reporting the real world. Which is vile cant. Kingsbury plays the game in a familiar (and quite unusually good-tempered) way. Without quite making it clear that this is the case, he rigs his Getan society so that its citizens have to be very accomplished at living in it to survive at all. Moreover, Getan society would patently fall apart in the absence of star winners like the members of the five-marriage who propel *Courtship Rite* along at such a breathtaking rate. Getan society — like most Libertarian societies in fiction — can only be *worked* by that tiny minority of people who are not only far more intelligent and creative and serendipitous and combat-ready and tough and horny and ruthless than any of us out here in the real world, but who also embody all these enticing attributes in a configuration that works precisely — *but only* — in terms of the society for which they have been created. And if the world is perfectly designed for those who can make that particular world work, who needs laws? Laws are for *losers*. Patting its victors on the back, it pats its own back. All others it eats.

So. As an ordinary person in a world that provides no clear moral or financial recompense for any behaviour at all, I began to feel slightly framed by *Courtship Rite*. But this could be a cheap suspicion on my part. I'm not about to claim that, for Donald Kingsbury, cannibalism is a proper extension of Social Darwinism. And none of this should muffle the central fact that the book is a considerable accomplishment, that it's a feast (of the imagination) and great fun while it lasted, within its covers, within its covers.

The Magazine of Fantasy and Science Fiction//December 1982

12//NW1//Ellison/Laumer/Kapp/Carter/Moorcock:

Shucksma

From Keith Laumer, Avram Davidson, Algis Budrys, Samuel R. Delany, Robert Sheckley, Theodore Sturgeon, Ben Bova, Robert Silverberg, A E van Vogt, William Rotsler, Joe L Hensley, Roger Zelazny, Robert Bloch and Henry Slesar, famed science fiction writer Harlan Ellison admits to having learned respectively strength, erudition, empathy, youthful commitment, outrageous madness, dazzlement and love, the rationality of reality, craft, complex conceptualization, irreverence, gentleness, poetic intricacy, the ability to come to grips with terror, and courage and pride and dignity so that, inevitably, a Heavy Dragoon is the residuum and indeed, as he later intimates in his priceless introduction to *Partners in Wonder* (Walker, 1971), a volume of his collaborations with Keith Laumer, Avram Davidson, Algis Budrys, Samuel R Delany and certain other authors, "only a fool or an amateur would consider working with them [see above], without a full realization of how good one must be to share the same story with each [ibid] of them," which deposition forces one into the realization that if Harlan Ellison is neither a fool nor an amateur, then he must be something else.

Speculation being invidious, however, we should keep ourselves to what the text at hand shows of an author who, as Donald A Wollheim uniquely phrased it in his *The Universe Makers*, "has indeed found new ultramodern ways of narration which yet manage to keep comprehension...," possibly at bay, for Ellison's high-pitched burning-bush prose is sometimes hard for an atheist to parse. Any author who claims, as he does in the same introduction, that failing in an attempt to compose a collaborative novel with Avram Davidson can claim to rank as an experience with "death camps, hard-hats, campus massacres and the human gamut that runs from Spiro to Manson," demonstrates, through the use of apocalyptic hyperbole as doodle, a sense of stylistic weighting that does rather burn the bush to the ground; the reader, kicking around in the ashes, isn't likely to find much more there than charred twigs, parboiled *shucksma* (a back-formation from "shucks Mother I dint mean to burn the garage down and crash the car and torture Pussy but aint I cute?") and carbonized fragments of Word. Nor is the author's claim at this point about Davidson and himself, that collaborations are risky enterprises, and that one can do just as well going it alone, much clarified when, on the following page, he advances the claim that successful collaboration is "akin to the benefits of sex with a partner," and that going it alone is like masturbation, and nobody has ever "gotten a baby by playing with himself." Brought together flapping their wings like drunken parrots, these two claims have an aching, vertiginous effect on the reader, rather like the effect of Ellison's best prose in general.

Comprised as it is of *shucksma* and vertigo, this prose forcibly reminds one of the iconography of the Italian Western, and relates in the same heated parasitic way to the genre from which it appropriates an excuse for tripping. It is the style of the dog-wagging tail — for however stiffly and ferociously erect the tail may be, its tumescence depends on the heart and arteries of the dog padding stoutly within networks of habit or genre, and it is in this way that the sort of story Harlan Ellison writes, with all its presumption of abandon (and consequent incoherence of affect [far too harsh, and inaccurate to boot: I should have said something like: and consequent whiplashes of affect *1986*]), finds itself in truth deeply bound to the genre which gives it sustenance, nor is it the case that he would deny this binding relation, for how else should one read his tribute to other writers in the field for what they've given him, from strength to dignity? Indeed the religiose excesses of the passages in which he tenders homage read as a fallacy of imitative form, a proof of the pudding.

Like Sergio Corbucci, Sergio Leone, Burt Kennedy, Ignazio F Iquino, Jose Maria Elorietta, Luigi Vanzi, Giovanni Simonelli, Gino Mancini, Camillo Mastrocinque and Antonio Isasi-Isasmendi, Harlan Ellison is a feeder, and it's not surprising to find that *Partners in Wonder*, whose introductory material we've been looking at, stands as by far the best of his collections [a really dumb judgement *1986*] to date. It does include one solo story, "The Prowler in the City at the Edge of the World," an item he has in any case already printed elsewhere more than once (in both *Dangerous Visions* and *Over the Edge* for starters), though that's a common science fiction practice, rooted in the gung-ho hothouse Alamo mentality of its market, for constant republication of stories wouldn't cut much marketing ice in the real world — but what the hell, it's one of his best efforts at "masturbation," and most of the volume's duos are either excellent or fascinating or both, showing their various senior collaborators off in splendid fashion, for Ellison has a distinctly vivifying influence on such writers as Van Vogt and Sheckley and even Silverberg, who sometimes, with all his skill and knowledge and sophistication, does tend to the androidal, so that a touch of the burning bush can be beneficial. What one reads, perhaps impolitely, as parasitism can, therefore, attain symbiosis, given the opportunity. The genre can only gain.

But back to the Alamo. Keith Laumer, a collaborator in *Partners*, has just released through Ballantine (1972) a new collection which he calls *Timetracks*, and indeed time travel or travel through dimensions does provide the jumping-off points or pretexts for several typical stories in the author's two veins: the licketysplit adventure romp with an affectless mercenary through time and space; and the "comic romp" with Retief or someone like him bamboozling a cast of gildersleeves or aliens (ie Coloured folk) without the law. Unfortunately for the reader with enough memory left to be allowed out of the hospital on weekends, most of the book has already appeared in other Laumer collections, and so recently that republication with a new publisher might seem a touch precipitate: "The Other Sky" in *Greylorn* (1968); and "The Time Thieves" (under a different title) in *It's a Mad, Mad, Mad Galaxy* (same year). These novelettes make up most of the bulk of *Timetracks*, so beware, not everyone can afford to be a science fiction reader.

The best nonhumorous Laumer novels and stories grip at one with manic panache through their stripping-away of everything irrelevant to the goal of arriving at a narrative embodiment of brute kinesis. Not only will the protagonist, usually an ego-neutral I, discard socialization, bourgeois responsibility and most other human affects, but in his search for what one might call kinetic invulnerability he will actually embed this mechanical self of his in the reality he so ominously prefigures, transforming himself or being transformed (as in *A Plague of Demons*) into an actual and invulnerable chassis fitted with weaponry-prosthetics. The reader finishes a book like this dizzy with a sense of momentum so perfectly aroused and sustained by the transformation of latent content into kinetic form that it will almost seem that he had been watching a genre movie which, with its wider attack on the sensorium, has tended to take kinesis over from the novel of adventure. Unfortunately, *Timetracks* presents a series of dead-ends, and when the transformation into a sentient tank is denied him Laumer is about as dreary a writer as anyone could imagine, a beached fanatic.

In the Alamo again, a writer with whom Harlan Ellison has not collaborated, Colin Kapp, bestows *The Patterns of Chaos* (Gollancz, 1972) upon the unwary, and its publisher doesn't help much by proclaiming that because it's "Full of big ideas, it will delight sf enthusiasts." Briefly as possible, *The Patterns of Chaos* is a kind of replay of Kapp's earlier attempt at creating that old genre standby, the hero who doesn't know who he is, only that the fate of the universe rests upon his discovering his identity and using his extraordinary powers, the earlier book being *Transfinite Man*, and a great deal more palatable than the current offering. Both are typical science fiction vulgarizations of the picaresque base paradigm — in which the boy/man without a family or homeland, the survivor, the agile picaro quests unceasingly for his true name, the name and identity of his father, and the location of his final home, where he will be at peace — for it is certainly not the case that the picaresque novel is formless and lacks direction; only the English distortions of the form, from Smollett to J B Priestley, are gormless .... In certain science fiction novels the base paradigm can go through a process of essentialization, for instance in Charles L Harness's *The Paradox Men*, where the amnesiac picaro protagonist, rebelling against a hostile world, discovers that he is his own father, and that he (as his father) is the hidden ruler of that hostile world, which had persecuted him just so long as he was not himself, and precisely for the reason that he was not himself. The climax of this book presents the deep message of the picaresque model with a clarity never achieved in its historical forms — know thyself, and the world is your oyster.

In *The Patterns of Chaos* the protagonist is duly amnesiac, but with a kind of clammy witlessness that also gums up much of the rest of this sorry claptrap the author fails at any point to explain *why*. As he goes about routinely expanding his powers, the protagonist merely happens to remember what it is convenient for the author to have him remember, and what the author wishes to remain blank in his hero's mind (because exposure would topple the book about its own ankles) remains blank, equally without explanation.

Bron, for that is the protagonist's burly moniker, possesses an inexplicable and ungovernable capacity to create chaos, and though by novel's end he is busily and traditionally engaged in the construction of a galactic federation *which he intends to run*, hardly the sort of thing an ungovernable entropy-increaser would be much shakes at, it is not for one to question the powers of amnesia, even the author's. But let's get to the *plot*: 600,000,000 or so years earlier, expert alien entropy-charters from far-off Andromeda, perceiving the threat ungovernable Bron would someday entail to their racial pride (that curse), have sent off a number of enormous planet-buster hellbombs on millenia-long courses designed to intersect with the burly one's path as he travels hither and yon creating chaos, the mind boggles, this takes half the book. Nothing loth to any sort of villany, moreover, Kapp's ancient Andromedans have, at the same time (600,000,000 years ago), possibly as an insurance against the failure of their flying bombs, *also* set off in a vast armada *at sublight speeds* on a millenia-long journey to conquer our home galaxy, all of it, and we are in the second half of the book, the entire galaxy is in danger, though just *when* and, considering the size of the galaxy and the sublight velocity of the dread armada, just *where* this threat can be thought to focus is made no clearer than the source of Bron's amnesia, which leaves one's suspension of disbelief riddled with credibility gaps, as though peppered by flying gnats.

But never mind, Bron games with entropy and duly decimates the Andromedans (who have wasted 600,000,000 years for nothing), and the plot begins to expand like a drunken zeppelin. Connected by improbable biolink to a sadistic female he can't remember who loves him and hates him at the same time from half a galaxy away in a subterranean bunker and who even though she is bitter and sophisticated and wryly wise and vicious manages to display a conversational style Kim Kinnison's fiancee would find hokey; and *additionally* connected by improbable biolink to a certain General Ananias who has trouble telling the truth, Bron hops into his parsec-cowing spaceship, and . . . .

What's the use, the book is impenetrable to sense and taste alike; one worries away at it mainly from a sort of flagellatory desire to work out how far authors and agents and publishers will permit themselves to go in a hothouse market — because it must be obvious that cynical and pernicious twaddle like *The Patterns of Chaos* could only be written and published for enclave suckers, that in the clearest possible sense it is a book for the addict, and that, as usual in this sort of enterprise, the shit is cut.

So the heart sinks, there are dozens of books at hand and to the blurred eye they all seem to be by Lloyd Biggle, Jr, to whom we gladly tender the favour of not reviewing *The Light That Never Was*, his newest and maybe his awfullest longueur, though closer examination of the stacks reveals that most of the piled volumes were, in fact, edited by Lin Carter, a cozy hothouse perennial if there ever was one, a writer who, to read the evidence he presents barrels of, has come to a parareligious conviction that Ballantine Books is in fact that great fanzine in the sky, and that it's going to get exactly what it deserves, from him. Not that the Adult Fantasy series hasn't disinterred a good number of worthy items — though it is true that Carter, in his fireside shovelfuls of chat, does evince a tendency to label authors "forgotten" as soon as he begins to remember them, to Ballantine's profit and to his. But it's the fanzine concept, which he embodies, of scholarship as an epiphenomenon of gossip, that best expresses his as it were deep-structural relation to the role of editor.

Discoveries in Fantasy (Ballantine, 1972), to take an example; the paragraph beginning on page 151 and ending overleaf. Editor Carter is talking about Eden Phillpotts, an author by no means forgotten in England. In his presentation of information he deems relevant, he fails to indicate that Phillpotts died as recently as 1960; fails to mention that his first novel was published in 1891 (not 1896) [his first book, incidentally, a collection of stories, appeared in 1888, which gives him a writing career almost as long as P G Wodehouse's *1986*]; that his last book appeared in 1959 (not 1954); and when he can think of no writer to have published a greater number of volumes than Phillpotts (some 250, he claims), he shows an ignorance of John Creasey (over 500 and alive [then] and famous) or Georges Simenon (around 500 and alive and even more famous) that would be forgivable in conversation but not in print, which is of course the great obvious essential lesson hothouse or enclave or Alamo buffs rarely seem to learn: that in the real world gossip cannot co-opt study [even on lowly matters like bibliography *1986*], nor chat substitute for thought.

Enclave cliques may once have been an adaptive response to a hostile environment, as Donald A Wollheim, the immortal platypus, claims in that prose he seems to think derives from H G Wells (page 20 of *The Universe Makers*, 1971), and as he cannot be paraphrased he must be quoted on those hardy Depression fans: "Our lives tended to be bent toward each other, our world was a microcosm of our own lives . . . ." How perfect, how plastic an expression of the inscrutability of fandom is that last phrase, how humbling for the congenital exile who has never been a fan to realize that he will *never understand* Donald A Wollheim; on my shelves, *The Universe Makers* will remain a closed book. [But see the next essay, on James Blish, to witness it reopened; I think I should note that the comic animus expressed in these two pieces against *The Universe Makers* had something to do with the Old Wave/New Wave schism still exciting some of us as late as 1972, and entered into with partisan vigour by Mr Wollheim in his history/survey of sf; granted, he was far more interested in "The Cosmogony of the Future," and in stories that dealt with "Human colonies on other starry systems" and the like, than in New Wave ambivalences about the toilet we shit in: but he did manage to lay on a diatribe or two, hence the counterattacking tone I took back then. *1986*] But the enclave simplex [Wollheim] embodies does linger on, though variously, as the novels and collections we've looked at hopefully demonstrate, and it begins to look more and more like an evolutionary cul-de-sac whose inhabitants increasingly resemble the magnificent splay-footed ostrich, especially when attempts are made to construct formal generic models for science fiction texts by writers and critics who don't lay eggs, scholars, for instance, like Darko Suvin, whose formalist review in the May 1972 issue of *The Magazine of Fantasy and Science Fiction* displays precisely the sort of cognition the field needs to survive, however one may judge particular points he makes [see next essay for comments on the inefficacy of Suvin's "cognitive estrangement" definition of echt-sf in attempting to understand the Gothic romance which, as Brian Aldiss argued with such clarity and panache in *Billion Year Spree*, 1973, is sf's Ur-form *1986*]. The time has come for a good deal of rethinking and hard work, but let Wollheim himself supply the peroration: "Grand adventure, which has had its followers when reprinted (as I have done in the sixties), but again, imitation without innovation must always remain shadowed by the work of the initiated."

Time for a brief coda, possibly embarrassing to Michael Moorcock, *New Worlds*'s editor, as it is in praise of his new novel, *Breakfast in the Ruins* (New English Library, 1972), which is no more science fiction than Vonnegut's *Slaughterhouse-Five*, nor as good for that matter. But precisely because writers identified with the science fiction genre are treated with distancing condescension by most critical outlets as products of an enclave, it's most unlikely that *Breakfast in the Ruins* will get review space outside the field, which is sufficient reason to touch on it here.

Most of Moorcock's oeuvre consists of sword and sorcery romances whose underlying sourness may raise them to a point where they could be described as albino camp, though not much further; but beyond these exercises in the invert thou, there are a number of increasingly substantial efforts whose relation to the fantasy and science fiction field has become more and more tenuous. Of these, *Breakfast in the Ruins* seems to be the cleanest and most austere example of Moorcock's attempts to write novels as such, though it would be going too far to claim that he's trying his hand [even now, in *1986*] at the bourgeois-individualist novel Joyce burned out.

Breakfast in the Ruins is subtitled "A Novel of Inhumanity," and is arranged as a series of paradigms, each paradigm laid out (or syntagmified) as an episode from the last 100 years of civilization whose structure requires the protagonist to make a moral choice about how he will survive; the implied desideratum is that the choice be humane, but within these paradigms the humane response is generally implausible, because of the nature of the world. A set of paradigms in Analyst's Couch sounds like a gabfest of episodes, and indeed the novel is only saved from disintegration by the use of a single protagonist, Karl Glogauer from *Behold the Man* (1969), whose successive incarnations advance him gradually in age, through time, and in the increasing difficulty of choice, so that his progress through the paradigms is a progress into corruption, but what else is there?

There is also a framing device which replicates the body of the novel: a homosexual Nigerian seduces the adult Glogauer, but is in turn seduced as the novel progresses, losing his survivor panache and his presumptive corruption to the increasingly "adept" Glogauer. This device, in any case a touch ramshackle, exhibits a curiously flat prose, a style unequal to the demands made upon it, and oddly inferior to what one finds in the body of the novel; it also echoes, rather unfortunately, the lubricity of the Jerry Cornelius books.

Though flawed and occasionally flat and possibly more intricate than necessary *Breakfast in the Ruins*, through the strength and mature indeterminacy of its emphasis on the constituent elements of moral choice in a gravely damaged social order, conveys a pervading melancholy that makes it vibrate to the perception with a strange, loaded poignancy, so that finally — rare praise — it is memorable.

New Worlds Quarterly 5//1973 (ie 1972)

13//NW2//James Blish:

Scholia, Seasoned with Crabs, Blish Is

[This essay/review appears in the slightly corrected shape it took on republication in Michael Moorcock's anthology, *New Worlds* (Flamingo Books, 1983). As a form of recognition of Blish's absorption in James Joyce, the first paragraph was composed to parody the first paragraph of *Ulysses*, and was, I hope, received by readers as registering an homage. But time passes, and scholarship alas recasts our nonage paradigms, and it should be noted that Garland Publishing's new critical edition of *Ulysses* (reissued with minor corrections and without scholarly apparatus by Random House and The Bodley Head in 1986) modifies even the first paragraph of that novel, so that Buck Mulligan's dressinggown is sustained *on* not *by* the mild morning air. It is a distinct improvement, but my version will not tolerate the shift, and so I retain, strictly for this reason alone, the old defective reading. The revised/corrected text of *Ulysses* is, by the way, beautifully set, and welcomes the reader in to this greatest novel *1986*.]

Stately, anfractuous James Blish comes down from Fabers, bearing a bowl of scholium on which two novels and a best sf of him lie crossed. Lyly's *Geology*, euphuistic Sod, is sustained gently behind him by the mild ignorant readership. He holds the bowl aloft and intones:

—The world's my *Ostrea edulis*.

Then closing the preface to his *Best Science Fiction Stories (Revised Edition)* with a sigh, down the dark winding stairs he comes to us with gifts, this grim scholar, fearful Jesuit, reaper of Joyce and biology, Strowger genre shifter (listen for the clunk) [even now the British telephone system features nineteenth century "Strowger" mechanical exchanges, which you can actually hear clicking out the number you've punched *1986*], misogynist qua texts, apocalypse lover with icy fingers, James Blish who devised the best template series science fiction had ever seen, the Okie series, and then ruined it, James Blish who now writes or operates the worst, *Star Trek*, and will not stop, James Blish, through whose corpus, as through a moraine, granite and guck interpenetrate cackling beneath the full moon, each new book a spastic *piñata* spewing delirious botched crab-apples forth, inedible cranky mutant gets, but then carved granite too, the death of God in *Black Easter*, John Amalfi's "slogging brutal tireless heart," the masked Menippean discourse kicking off *A Case of Conscience*, the Kodiak bear terminating *The Warriors of Day* with a sudden salutary perspective transform, so that in dealing with this most uneven of all major writers of science fiction one never quite knows what to expect next in the dark, quicksand or a bed of nails.

The books on hand ostensibly for review — Faber's three (*Best Science Fiction Stories, The Day After Judgement, And All the Stars a Stage*) which make up a bag sufficiently mixed to be sold only on prescription; plus *Midsummer Century*, a 35,000 word story optimistically bound by Doubleday between hard covers nearly as thick as the text and including a list of Blish's publications nearly as long; and finally a Penguin release of the superb *Black Easter* from 1968 — all go a long way to increase the confusion in breast and head, make more urgent the job of dissevering joy from glop. But there is always a silver lining. Difficulties of gist apprehension, and general fibrillation of the affect, are not in this case intensified by any delirium parataxis from the pen of Donald A Wollheim as wielded with his thumb throughout *The Universe Makers*, that inimitable fan's vade-mecum for the sniffing out of sf security risks ("The New Wave represents a departure from the science fiction directives for mankind") and for the identification of echt-sf on the high road of "Future Predictions" ("that framework of millions of years to come"), through his expedient refusal to mention James Blish at all. Blish leans to dystopic versions of the future, to rebarbative excursions into moral philosophy, and to apocalypses both frigid and terminal; Wollheim ("Humanity, whatever its faults, is the best darned thing going and will never be pinned to the mat") does not. Perhaps it is for that reason that the raven of DAW has excluded, from his conspectus of the *mind-boggling futures* science fiction is directing us into, any reference to the works of James Blish, inventor of the spindizzy, and flying cities, and consequential models of galactic commerce, and pantropy seeding the spread stars. Certainly it is the case that Mr Wollheim trucks little with moral ambiguities and shades of 20th Cent Grey (copyright pending), for, as he puts it, in his own words:

> *Good* lives!
>
> What does it mean when a thirst for novels wherein unmistakable heroes fight against unmistakable villains continues to show itself in fantasy writings . . . ?
>
> It means that there is hope for humanity and hope for youth. For it means that hundreds of thousands — possibly millions — of young intelligent people are not basically cynics and victims of despair. It means that the ancient belief in the rightness of innate Good — that belief which sustained all the armies of prehistory whose battles laid the foundations for all that we call civilization and culture — has not died from the human spirit. Youth recognized it when it came to them in its ancient pure form and rallied to it.
>
> Let the New Wave sneer and snarl and cry that science fiction is dead and its vision of galactic futures dead; let them present their writings of despair filled with shock words and shock concepts; they have been defeated already by the cry *Frodo Lives!*

Some critics — possibly James Blish himself — might discover objections to this remarkable reading of the social consequences of pretending to believe in Frodo buttons, and might interpret the extraordinary popularity of *The Lord of the Rings*, whose author in any case explicitly repudiated any attempt to allegorize his romance, as a sign not of moral rearmament but of its reverse, not "belief in the rightness of innate Good" but "shock words and shock concepts" like the growing sense, not solely ecological, that we are the toilet we shit in.

The dejuiced angsty nostalgia for icons that so clearly riddles Frodomania — they might argue — bears a signifying relation to the post-industrial quietism currently infusing modern youth's bosom with repressively-desublimated Orexis Rot, and the same signification must surely apply to those weenybopper theosophies more recently woven, with dank cabbalistic bootlicking and Art Nouveau cartoons, around the sword and sorcery fantasies of Michael Moorcock, for which he must take some blame, as he does not stop writing them, and has in consequence become a purple sage. In their easy desolateness these fantasies represent — one supposes — a *Star Trek* of the inscape, and in their firm bleached contours and carious irreality they provide decals galore for icon-building; nor, in a world that feels the need for forms of belief, but has generally lost the innocence to believe in the forms of belief, should that accomplishment be counted negligible, just maybe a touch chilling ....

Icon-wise, as we shall see, James Blish has a brown thumb, nor is he cheerful, so it is no more surprising to note his failure to build a consistent version of himself for the field to chew on, like Heinlein's, than it is to recollect his exclusion from former Ace kingpin Wollheim's shortlist of future-builders of good faith, which includes guys like Mark S Geston, and Alexei Panshin, and Dean R Koontz, and A Bertram Chandler, and Andre Norton (gal).

Even a selective glance at Blish's oeuvre, none of which ever appeared in Ace Books, demonstrates a formidable yet strangely ill-at-ease range and industry and craft: take *The Warriors of Day* (1951), for instance, or *Jack of Eagles* (1952), both impregnated with pulp but natty; or *Cities in Flight* (1950-1962), inside the avoirdupois of which a template saga begs to be let out, *pace* Spengler, as English readers will at last be able to confirm (or deny) for a small sum early in 1974, when Arrow Books will be publishing the whole sequence in paperback. Speaking of templates (Blish's own term, by the way), Arrow will also be releasing later this year the first three or four volumes of the Dumarest series, E C Tubb's fine, modest, rounded, professional quest-for-Earth sequence [which, as the years passed, would extend into dozens of volumes, each succeeding instalment marginally less well-knit than its predecessor; the sequence has finally become a kind of object lesson in how not to capitalize on the technical interminability of the template form *1986*].

Or take *A Case of Conscience* (1953-1958), the embedded tone- and affect-clarity of whose initial discourse strikes — suggestively — a note of fitness of means to intention lacking elsewhere in the list; or *The Seedling Stars* (stories assembled in 1957), in which pantropy and a sketchy galactic colonization model get too brief a run but live beyond their text.

Or take *VOR* (1949-1958), a misshapen effort, as Damon Knight has shown, a monster story whose peculiarly disgruntled and — as it were — *low-budget* adherence to sidelines of the action nicely illuminates a seedier aspect of genre construction. One might call it the *metonymy con*, and refer to its frequent illustration in B movies, where budgetary nightmares like car crashes or the end of the world demand avoidance gambits in which a rhetoric of personalized response and simplified gesture will substitute for any attempt at rendering the complex (or expensive) action. It all results in a miniaturized, claustrophobic, sidelined, papier-mache world, whose protagonists invariably and most oddly seem half-blinded by flashbulbs, nor are there shadows. A typical shot sequence is (we insist) triadic. First (after the quarrel) there is the quick scared look of outward regard, preferably on the part of the hero, optionally succeeded (second) by a nerve-shatteringly swift eyeline shot of a Dinky Toy totalling against a twig, and concluded (third) by three lollygagging minutes of *con* that comprise the heart of the avoidance gambit — this being an interminable reaction shot synecdoche in which the heroine, leaning against a cardboard tree, nags at the protagonist in a shrill, contemptuously "feminine" monologue until we could all just scream. What do you *mean* Los Angeles is doomed, Harry, what are you *talking* about it's the end of the world, Harry. You're being ridiculous, Harry, and *mean*, and you don't love me. My father, Senator Higginbotham, who is your father-in-law, Harry, he said there was nothing to worry about, Harry, and *he* wouldn't lie, though I don't expect you to believe that. Harry, I won't *go!* This Hollywood misogyny — which James Blish has indulged himself in more than once, viz. Dee Hazelton — neatly conforms to another conveniently low-budget conceit — which Mr Blish has also made use of, viz. *They Shall Have Stars* — the idea that the audience somehow longs to identify with (and feel marginally superior to) that generic humour known as the Most Ignorant Participant, who is usually female, and that it therefore welcomes any chance it is given to be told, at stupefying length, facts which, out of the entire cast, she and only she persists in failing to comprehend.

Or take *Titan's* — also listed as *Titans'* — *Daughter* (1952-1961), a book which seems misnamed wherever its publisher places the apostrophe, as the girl in question, though eight feet tall, and the close friend of other, taller, better-informed, more important Titans, can claim neither to be the story's protagonist nor the daughter of anyone at all large. More interestingly, however, *Titan's Daughter* is a bumpy, peremptory compendium of narrative dislocations and affect discords, a chilled and chilling demonstration of its author's characteristic impatience with that mimesis of temporal continuity and beingness even sf tropes call for, if a novel is intended, and not something else.

Then take *The Star Dwellers* (1961), one of those horrifying juveniles whose protagonist (usually some sort of ROTC thug) saves Terra, and everyone who lives thereon, through being *liked* by some alien or other sitting in judgment on us all. This one additionally features a saucy teenage girl reporter who, like Good Fellowship in a morality, pops in and out of sight *just as though* she were fulfilling an exemplary function — but the story has no thesis she can illustrate, and the action unfolds as though she were not present. There is a lesson to be learned from this.

Or take *The Night Shapes* (1962), a parody, perhaps not quite sufficiently affectionate, though admirably deadpan, of Haggard Burroughs and Co's melodramatic wet-dreams of Armed Innocence turned loose to wreak vengeance on all cowardly natives, venomous beasts, craven Arabs — and on the tit-flaunting Princess, whose inner corruption and staple diet, dilled testicle, clues one in to the fact that she, and every one of her attendant natives beasts and foreigners, functions in the text as an *earth*, and in this way whitewashes "Tarzan's" otherwise inadmissible Id. In all of this an uglier form of metonymy holds sway, that form of the con otherwise defined as scapegoating. Philip José Farmer has even more cogently handled the wetdream of the omnipotent Id by making *his* Tarzan *literally* all penis, penis dentata, though it must be admitted that Mr Farmer gives to *A Feast Unknown* rather too convincing an appearance of conviction, an appearance Mr Blish effortlessly manages to avoid conveying in *The Night Shapes*. I read the book, incidentally, as a parallel worlds novel, feeling pretty ingenious as I did, and basing my analysis on certain "errors" that proliferated through the first pages of the text. Lyly, author of *Euphues* (1578), was presented as the author of the "newly-published *Elements of Geology*," while in *this* world its author was Sir Charles Lyell, its title *Principles of Geology*, and its date of publication a generation or two prior to the time of the novel, which I took to be around 1904-1905. And H Rider Haggard, nearly fifty in 1904, was referred to as "young Haggaard," which also seemed otherworldly enough, even led tentatively to an Afrikaans hypothesis . . . . But all in vain. Mr Blish has since indicated (personal conversation, 27 January 1973) that the subtle distortions and hints I had nosed out were nothing more than author's slips, or typos, or printer's errors; the parody was this-worldly. Exegesis bit the dust of the jumble of the mere world.

Or take any of the books ostensibly on review.

Take the vast *faux-naif* ungainly array of generic conventions their author lays on and yanks off, or the affect shambles he so often creates with an arbitrary curtain or an icy stiff-kneed dismissal (like Chris deFord's in *Earthman, Come Home*), or the abiding sense of unease created in the reader by each book's determined avoidance of narrative equipoise, and a unifying conclusion will slowly force itself into view: that we have been traducing intelligent, scholarly, didactic James Blish by considering him a writer of novels at all, nor should that realization read as pejorative.

Blinkered by a vocabulary both procrustean and shambolically vague, and tactically constrained by a Germanic obsession with anything triune, literary critics have for centuries tended to define all prose fictions as novels (with drama and poetry as the second and third communicants in the trinity), and to derive further generic classifications (like angelic hosts) from that initial act of subsumption, so that we have learned to speak (and think) of realistic novels, and autobiographical novels, and science fiction novels, and fantasy novels, and satirical novels, and utopian novels, and so on, re-enacting the primordial fiat like mad cookiecutters, and picking our teeth clean of a lot of mangled Bunyan and Swift and Peacock and Huxley and — right — James Blish as we proceeded, too. That this will no longer do I am not precisely the first to note, nor has the triune hypostasy that generates it only recently become a matter for ribaldry, and so I claim no originality for the impressionistic hints that follow, some of which are based on an attempt to comprehend Northrop Frye, and which are pale suns of that father.

In his *Beyond Genre* (1972), Paul Hernadi takes on and presents for contemporary readers Ramon Fernandez's 1926 proposal to divide prose fictions into two broad tonalities or aspects. At one pole, the *roman* concerns itself with "the representation of events as they emerge and develop in time." Its "intuitive," "synthetic," "vital tonality evokes a 'psychological present' (which has nothing to do with the grammatical tense of a text)." This idiom, the idiom of the *roman*, is clearly instinct with and generates mimesis. At the other pole, the *recit* concerns itself with "the presentation of past events by a narrator in accordance with the principles of logic and rhetoric." Its "logical" and "analytical" tonality reports a "conceptualized *temps*," which has nothing to do with grammatical tense either, but which gives off a sense of distanced, disjunct pastness. This idiom, the idiom of the *recit*, is just as clearly instinct with and generates exemplification.

Avoiding category errors like the plague (because the *roman/recit* polarity is tonal not formal, and because we have been taught to be neat), we can see that the traditional novel, as hypostasized by the triune hierophants, is in fact a *roman* — warm, plastic, representational, *seamless*, lacking any coarse " 'holes' in the fabric of time," as Dr

Hernadi goes on to say — and that fictions in the *recit* idiom will read as being chilly, didactic, presentational, disjunctive, *full of arbitrary lacunae in the quilt of space*, will read in other words as deficient *romans*, and will be assigned to the charnel where Procrustes dumps his legs.

Most of our great novelists have written in the *roman* tradition, it is true, though their fictions bear rather less structural resemblance to each other than one might have guessed from the rubric they bear in common. Fielding, or Richardson, or Smollett (but not Sterne), or Dickens (but not Meredith), can be so read without much discomfort. Nearing our own century, however, the identification of "novel" and *roman* gets more and more ludicrous, and becomes a formula for the writing of midcult kitsch most serious authors simply fail any more to observe — cf. Joyce, or Mann, or Proust (but not Maugham), or Faulkner (but not dear Saul Bellow). Still further on, taking a fiction the old vocabulary simply flenses, Nabokov's *Pale Fire* (1962) is a "novel" whose tonal idiom might well be rendered as genuine *recit* pretending to be a fake *recit* pretending to be closet *roman*.

And back with James Blish, we're able to dissolve some of the knots and crabbed access he offers to the field through the realization that, as a writer, he is deeply immersed in the *recit* idiom, maugre science fiction's general devotion to a shrill, streamlined mimetic parlance. As his fictions are radically deficient by *roman* canons, their fitness to a less popular idiom seems genuinely redemptive, for the critic. Blish's incapacity at the shaping of a mimesis of time's present tense in the work, and his compulsively frigid vetoing of any of his characters' movements towards intersubjectivity or joy, now seem — in this new reading — valid assays at a different task, the exemplification of dystopic topoi dear to the *recit* mind, like Voltaire's or Swift's, the pointing of a lesson through exemplary catastrophes, exemplary discourse, through exemplary characters and diction and mise en scene — though we're still left with the job of formally defining the fictions through which these dystopias are rendered, because certainly we cannot go on calling them novels.

In the Fourth Essay of his *Anatomy of Criticism* (1957), Northrop Frye divides prose fictions into four categories: the novel, which began in the eighteenth century and continued into ours, though now dead, and from which most *Great Traditions* select their mash; the romance, whose "stylized" protagonists "expand into psychological archetypes," and which "often radiates a glow of subjective intensity that the novel lacks," so that there should be no doubt where most science fiction fits snugly in; the confession, which includes autobiographies, but also that "introverted" and "intellectualized" form of fiction concerned with integrating a life and the thoughts that make it "worth writing about," a description which might be of some help in the long overdue rehabilitation of the later H G Wells; and finally the Menippean satire or anatomy (or icicle), which James Blish does not always write, but possibly always wants to.

> The Menippean satire [says Professor Frye] deals less with people as such than with mental attitudes. Pedants, bigots, cranks ... rapacious and incompetent professional men of all kinds, are handled in terms of their occupational approach to life as distinct from their social behaviour. The Menippean satire thus resembles the confession in its ability to handle abstract ideas and theories, and differs from the novel in its characterization, which is stylized rather than naturalistic, and presents people as mouthpieces of the ideas they represent .... At its most concentrated [it] presents us with a vision of the world in terms of a single intellectual pattern. The intellectual structure built up from the story makes for violent dislocations in the customary logic of narrative, though the appearance of carelessness that results reflects only the carelessness of the reader or his tendency to judge by a novel-centered conception of fiction.

So — as varyingly for Swift, Thomas Love Peacock, the very last things of Wells, for Aldous Huxley, Wyndham Lewis, John Barth, David Stacton, Thomas M Disch and John T Sladek — tonal and formal distinctions fuse neatly into a cage for James Blish, whose *recit* mind longs for a cold bath of Menippus to shape its grasp, or so we've been claiming. Unfortunately Mr Blish has immersed himself in a field — science fiction — whose generic forms are offspring of the heated iconicity of the romance, as stripped down for action, and his whole crabby yawing corpus demonstrates the cost of writing against the grain.

A further minatory scouring of the serried cross-grained ranks of his work might, therefore, seem a touch gratuitous, though the cage or model does cast a few broad heuristic shafts of light. Blish's enormous distance, as implied narrator, from the exemplary worlds or dissertations he creates, does come clear; as does the scholarly brambling of texts with spinoffs of scholia introduced as their own ends; as does his apparent need to create evolutionary sequences rather than templates (by which I mean exemplary sequences rather than fluvial, not temporal sequences as opposed to static ones), which cost *Cities in Flight* its nous, and which segues into a love of the admonitory catastrophe; as does his revealing attempts to subsume disparate texts under post facto rubrics (cf. *After Such Knowledge*); as does his gloom, which is not inhumane, but which is not — a quality Kenneth Rexroth anyway ascribes only to the very greatest flowerings of the novel tradition — magnanimous, either; as does the false innocence that permeates his fictions, as it permeates the works of all *recit* authors, and which abides in the realization that thematically naive topoi are being required — disingenuously — to illustrate far more than they could possibly *mean* to; and finally the nature of our assent to his successful fictions (like *A Case of Conscience*) does come clearer, for it is an assent to equipoise of assertion not narrative, conveyed through structures in space, not time, and recollected as models, not habitations.

As a Menippean illustration of the hypothesis that black magic literally works, *Black Easter* (1968), one of the books this is all in aid of a review of, might seem altogether stripped to its skeleton, but in the event the emperor is dressed. Characters and plot are so closely and economically bound to their task of demonstration, and the narrative is so elegantly short, that there is a kind of paronomasia — a kind of "blessedness" — and a dystopic thesis laves us in the clothes of *fleuve*. Its sequel, *The Day After Judgement* (1970) is a disjointed, cack-handed anticlimax, and de-frissons the death of God in *Black Easter* by allowing that He might only be on vacation and be putting Satan on His throne pro tem, because Nature abhors a vacuum — which makes it the *real* shaggy God story. In its use of metonymy cons both of character and of narrative it's as miniaturizingly evasive as *VOR*; in its generic chuntering about it's as loopy as *Titan's Daughter*; and in the *Malleus Maleficarum* misogyny it shares with its predecessor it is thoroughly egregious.

And All the Stars a Stage (1960-1972), a grim and jumbled melange, starts off as a juvenile and closes, to coin a term, as a *senile*. For a while it's a matriarchal dystopia (in Blish's universe, matriarchy and dystopia are synonyms) set on a world we do not know; then it becomes an end-of-the-world story, whose protagonists escape into space in the nick of time, leaving behind them the usual squalid prole mobs; then it's a quest-for-a-new-home-through-vast-reaches-of-the-galaxy story, during which (to validate the title) we get occasional querulous glimpses of a cardboard star or two, and during which the heroes make educational visits to various strange planets; and finally it becomes an arrival-at-New-Jerusalem-kiss-the-soil-kids story, rather neat though muffled by lack of space. The new home turns out to be Earth, and the genuinely best thing in the book is its superb closing sentence. Not for the first time in Blish's oeuvre, women composers are calumniated (page 99), and "simple male pride" (page 43) gets over its dose of dystopia late in the book when Ailiss, once a female dominant (but now a wife), refuses to take over command of the ship when the clear duty to do so falls upon her, because at the last moment her feminine intuition has recognized the natural order of things. "I will *not*," she says, possibly in that *dangerously even* tone of voice so characteristic of Doris Day, "I will *not* be in command over my own husband — not at my age."

In *Midsummer Century* (1972) a man's mind is accidentally disembodied and cast far into the future where, linked to a second discorporate intellect, it gets the chance to observe and comment on a variety of Dying Earth dystopias, while time passes. In other words, Blish has structurally disjuncted his protagonist from the exempla of the text, and has allied — affianced — him to the functions of the implied narrator, so that he becomes no more — nor less — than a syntax of vision, all of which seems so clarifying a demonstration of the nature of the *recit* perspective that the book might well have been titled *The Eye of Menippus*. Although a clubfooted adventure plot does welsh on this version of a Garden, what there is of this storyline does eventually wander back off-stage, and the calm distant rather melancholy pleasures return, literally embodying, in a sort of pun, what Darko Suvin terms, in his attempt to define sf, "cognitive estrangement," a term he seems to intend to use as a monothetic purge of the field as a whole, but which seems to work best as a modelling device for the closer description of the Menippean form of the genre — and not of its dominant romance forms, because cognitive estrangement blights the icon.

And Frodo expires belike.

But our nostalgia (our need) for the steamy, high-pitched, kinetic fatefulness of iconicity persists, for genres work (human perception works) not only through metonymy, the substitution of part for whole, of set for omniscience dreams, but also through the persistence of the image, time's body English. "Fatefulness," says Erving Goffman in *Interaction Ritual* (1967), "involves a play of events that can be initiated and realized in a space and time small enough to be fully witnessed." Icons are torsions in time, which heats them, and gives them pull through the work. Fate is mimed before us, in a matrix co-extensive with vision's. The anatomy shrivels icon to juggle metonymy for the cold eye, hence James Blish draped in icicles; the romance swallows metonymy neat that icons may live, Frodo lives. Pray for light. The hero of romance ubsumes metonymy (being rather dumb) and mimes fate's glow, time's abric's meshing with the ganglia of the icons of our hot breath, and hat is meet.

*Vew Worlds Quarterly 6/in USA New Worlds Quarterly 5//*1973 (ie 1972)

14//NW3//Brian W Aldiss:

I Say Begone! Apotropaic Narcosis, I'm Going to Read the Damned Thing, Ha Ha

[Brian Aldiss has had a very large career, and it's been unlucky for me that I've missed reviewing so many of his best books — not having had the chance to give any sort of notice in print to *An Age* or *Frankenstein Unbound* or *The Malacia Tapestry* or *Moreau's Other Island*, to name only some of the more recent novels. A short bodged review of *The Saliva Tree* appeared in the Toronto *Star* in 1966, and a positive response to *Barefoot in the Head* surfaced in *New Worlds* three years later, but both items were too scruffy to reprint here. Highly positive reviews of *Helliconia Summer* showed up in *Omni* and *The New Scientist*, but they were short impersonal pieces, not the sort of copy one wants to hoick into permanent form. And just this year, in the *Times Literary Supplement*, a rather more extended piece, on *Trillion Year Spree: The History of Science Fiction*, did appear, and (in part) attempted to exculpate Aldiss from the laming impact of his collaborator's jejune coverage of recent books: but that review does not fit into this volume. What remains is the fantastico/theoretical essay printed below, with all its excesses of rudeness and vituperation about one terrible book — and subtextual prayer to an author one respected (and respects) to please *not* bugger about, because the fall from grace is so much more visible in the likes of Mr Aldiss, given the grave ironic sweep of his natural voice, the unhouseling gravitas of his larger vision *1986.*]

One hell of a lot deeper than plummet sounds into *The Eighty-Minute Hour*, Brian W Aldiss's emphysematous new science fiction space opera spoof about the genre's heatdeath and maybe his persona's likewise, the reader with true grit will finally come across a few interesting pages, and may feel, in consequence, and absurd gratitude on noting their presence in this distressing text from a significant author (1974) and Jonathan Cape (£2.25). I felt absurdly grateful. The passages of interest occur toward the end of a running parody of sword-and-sorcery-opera which Aldiss has interweaved — in alternate chapters — with the main substance of the book, in a sort of epistemological guying of the convention of the *deadpan multiverse*, a marketing device (Miss Eternal Return? I'd like you to meet Einstein Waffle — no petting now!) which flings together miscellaneous bumpf looted from anthropology and comparative religion in order to resuscitate sequence heroes killed off too soon by authors bored to catatonia by — say — Julliann of the Sharkskin and his horse Morngloom of mimsy pastel, manureless.

The Sword-and-Sorcery-Opera-of-the-Multiverse's peneplain exiguity of content; the glum and weedy kitsch of its dialogue conventions; the deep moroseness underlying those arbitrary changes of venue (uh, structure is like metaphor) endemic to this subliterature, whose typical reader might well be described, in marketing terms, as a Noumena Wanker: these characteristics, in his passages of some interest, Aldiss sends up by moderately intensifying them, and because in these passages (alone) he controls his voice, his multiverse parody comprises the most accessible and enjoyable line of narrative assault in *The Eighty-Minute Hour.* By the time our (forthcoming) quotation from the book comes around, moreover, Aldiss is just about to snap shut his epistemological gape and reveal the fact that the hero of his parody — Julliann of the Sharkskin himself — inhabits not a multiverse but a mere drug-induced fantasy, that his true name is simply Julian, that he is a legless sourpuss living in a San Diego slum in a world nearing apocalypse, and that he is related to some of the circumambient novel's ostensible protagonists, the last and least of whom, Durrant Surinat, also legless but more cheery about it, presumably narrates the whole caboodle in the first person. Narrative omniscience is thus eschewed, but mainly in the breach. Indeed, so transparent is Durrant Surinat, palimpsest-wise, and so effortlessly identical with the voice of the implied author (who may have no logical existence beyond the text, cf Wayne Booth's *Rhetoric of Fiction*, but who is still the only Brian W Aldiss most readers will ever perceive), that one often quite forgets the jolly amputee for chapters on end of his claimed narration, and may be forgiven the suspicion that the implied author — "Aldiss" if not Aldiss *pur* — had done likewise, Durrant Surinat coming therefore less as a guise of the author than as a scrim for same, through which a terrifying cachinnation urps, but more of that in a moment.

Right now it's the last lap of Julliann of the Sharkskin's multiverse hegira, and here he is, having come into sight of his castle which is yclept Slot Surinat, and (lo!) yet another danger confronts him, a grey fogbank which one of his dire companions identifies (before the rest of them charge into it) as "The Dread Brain Mist," a locution whose hectoring jocosity urps forth (to re-locute an insulting verb) elsewhere in the book, too, like a voiceprint, and whose manic abruption into the multiverse parody augurs that closing-in of the "real world," that snapping shut of the epistemological gape I've already described, praising it, in theory.

Round about here Durrant, who is little more than precisely a voiceprint, takes over to tell us that the Mist is "an evil phantom that had haunted man ever since the first men set foot on any version of Earth, Early, Middle, Late or Overdue," and the peculiar awfulness of this quote deserves some comment. Note first the semantic shift from "man" to "men" *within* a semantic moment, a shift from hypostasis to actual-figures-in-the-mind's-eye, however vaguely seen, which results in a fine example of misplaced concreteness — although "man" may inhabit a version of Earth without straining the overriding diction of this quote, when "the first men set *foot* on a *version* of Earth," the reader tends to suffer from that heat-haze of the syntax immemorially generative of Stuffed Owls or, when unfunny, vertigo. Note also that the dissonant near-repetition of "man" in "men" offends the ear, too. And note the general turkey-like gobble of clunk-eared syllables from the "phan" in "phantom" to "ver" in "version," like a goods train braking down a sharp grade, dum-uh-de-dum. And note, finally, the appalling punchline on "Overdue," after reading which one's ribs ache from the finger; it's the sort of joke possibly worth a stray guffaw if delivered ad lib to fans at a convention, but which is only distressful in print, though at the same time it does offer some illumination (of which more in a moment) on the problem (a problem shared by enclave literatures and Elks) of how the implied author relates to his readership.

But to continue.

Back to the Dread Brain Mist, which turns out to be "a desolating and supine thing" going "under many names such as estrangement, infirmity, melancholy, indecision . . . " — plus twenty-eight further substantives to the effect that "ALL IS NOT WELL!" Caught in the Mist, Julliann loses sight of his companions and his horse dies, going "to join its equine ancestors in the Celestial Stables." (Joke.) Trapped in the tacky labyrinth, Julliann is soon completely disoriented:

> Only then did he realize that the Dread Brain Mist had formed about him in a gigantic analogue of his own mind. Now he understood why Gururn and Harry had disappeared — by now, they also would be enveloped and swallowed by their own brains. When understanding came to him, faded frescoes appeared on the walls, their colours often muted, their meanings often lost; only occasionally did a scene stand out as brightly as once it had done. Here was his whole life, scene by scene, and he passed each scene cursing. Each was disappointing, the figures in it shrunken and misshapen, the incidents ridiculous, the protagonists ill-briefed for their roles — and the roles in any case minor and fragmentary, things that had to be hurried through, unrehearsed, and generally with nobody watching.

Making an element of a book physically analogous to its protagonist's mind can pay off both as an esemplasy releaser (within the text we perceive) and as a ground for paraphrasis (short of allegory) in a novel like Pär Lagerkvist's tightly through-composed *Barabbas* (1950), where the device as such may well have taken on the "detachable" form that Michael Moorcock slightly overspecified in *The Final Programme* (1965 in *New Worlds*); in the hands of the implied Aldiss's cursory Durrant, however, this device pays off only as paraphrastic of the question whose utterance exhausts it, to wit: *Whose mind?*

Whose is Durrant's voice?

From what rhetorical matrix does that melancholy hee-haw tickle our ribs?

If the implied author's "mind" is nothing more or less than precisely the book that embodies it, have we then been witness to a *confession?*

Who's the priest?

Immediately after the quote we've taken, Aldiss repeats verbatim (hee guys, haw guys) the list of thirty-odd substantives descriptive of the Dread Brain Mist, calling them "wry intimations of" Julliann's "human state"; and then, deeply depressed, Julliann intones a poem ("Our lives are stews of legend, evermore, / Re-heated and re-served by patterned lore") rather less Pynchonesque than most of the others Aldiss inserts throughout the book (apparently as a play on space "opera"), but just as patently a foregrounding device as any of them, underlining once more the central problem of this text: the decipherment of voice, which of course involves *placing* it.

At this point, Julliann's depression worsens:

> His sword dropped from his strong right hand, so full of misery was he, tramping blindly through corridors he had already trod, never knowing what was round the next corridor.

Nor is that all; the sense that the corridors Julliann treads are analogous to the reader's course through the novel itself (most of whose plot we have not yet tried to describe) by no means loses force on the next page when the voice of the book claims (or confesses to) an analogy between Julliann and the author himself, for author and text are homologous:

> Cowardly, wretched, unarmed — however low the state to which his present misfortune had reduced him, Julliann continued against all discouragement, much like an author nearing the end of a chronicle he believes nobody will peruse, yet bent on having one last jest at the expense of non-existent readers.

. . . Which adds to the question *Whose mind?* the equally important Siamese rider, *What readers?* — because I don't for a moment believe that Mr Aldiss really thinks he's not going to have them. On the contrary. Throughout this shambles of a book (synopsis follows), the voice of the implied Aldiss addresses itself conformally to a clear model of readership — a readership guaranteed to absorb *The Eighty-Minute Hour* at some level or other. It will come as no surprise at this point if one identifies that model of readership as a composition of fans, and the matrix, within which the voice of the book's telling takes place, as a rhetoric of connivance (or Alamo Bee) binding implied author to implied fan.

OK.

At an sf convention, the relation between author and fan may arguably resemble jazz and storytelling, two familiar stagings of communication as an interactive process which do in fact resemble each other, though neither much resembles a book . . . . Like convention highs, both are sessions. In jazz there is (or can be) a working rhetoric of communion between the claimed spontaneity or presentness-to-input of the performer, and the nature of the audience, comprised as it is of those "fatefully" *seen* to be present; both interact to shape the session, nor can that session either be repeated or paraphrased: hence our intuitive that it is something holy (man). In oral storytelling, the same "fateful" presentness of ground to focus, and focus to ground, bears a semantic burden as well, for the teller of the tale lays on vicarious destinies whose outcomes are responded to as being *perceivably* related to that ground which is the audience, which is the community. The teller is the voice we know; his formulaic web prefigures generic topoi, which may explain some of the confusion of rhetorical voice in modern sf (and Delany's Mouse). The storyteller's pauses and melismas and hints and cocoricos mediate any awkward caesuras, improbabilities, slack portions of narrative or genealogy, digressions from the shape of the ground that lends an ear; sanctioning the tale by the tone of its telling, he keeps fate in trim: seen but not paraphrasable: always under the sign of the session, where the teller is not defined as priest (putting out all over the sacred ground) but as known voice, relating.

And so an author en famille at the Alamo . . . .

But try to shift this rhetoric of communion into the matrix of a book's voice (as in *The Eighty-Minute Hour*, for instance, or in *Nova*) simply and fundamentally cannot succeed, for a book is not a session, nor does its implied author genuinely communicate with hypostasised fans, because he (the shape of the implied Aldiss) precisely is the text itself (as we've already claimed), all else being ventriloquism. Having dreamed the incompossible fan, the implied Aldiss (like Theodore Sturgeon and Robert A Heinlein and Samuel R Delany) must take responsibility for any gaffes engendered by that false relation; authorship as an oration to fans confuses composition with performance, and creates that rhetoric of connivance with which the reader (a real fan say) may well be complicit, because it seems flattering, but which ultimately grates the teeth. Nor are the perspectives of time (as in the weekend essays of Maurice Hewlett, to really lay it on) very kind to the *pathos* of connivance claims.

So the implied Aldiss must take responsibility for all the noise and all the gaffes of the book under review; for all the hectoring and nudge-nudge-wink-winking and drawn-out punning ("A big woolly lamb trundled by. It too was smiling. Sheepishly."); for the Thorne Smith filibustering ("There was a glacier parked in the car park. More than parked, in fact. It covered most of the park . . ." and so on and so on), so narcotic, so time-killing, as reminiscent of the 1960s Murray Leinster as of the author of *Topper*; for tone-deaf grammar (". . . to bear convincingly tidings . . .") and for grammar simply wrong ("A slight comedy goes among the other two most noted guests . . ."); for flyblown ("Half his cranium and the top of his face had been sliced off — not wisely, maybe, but too well.") gusto; for lumbering oxymorons ("Their presence filled the absent rooms.") and goosed figures — get it? — of speech (". . . a herring of deepest redness . . .") and shambling personifications ("... Nature, ever sly to make a come-back...") — all of which an oral storyteller or speechifier might possibly get away with through his manipulative sussing of the encounter, through his *stagecraft*, but which a book can't. Finally, in the solitude of his true nature, this "Brian W Aldiss," this book's voice must take responsibility for that distressing pathos we've already adduced, that indecorous confusion between stagecraft and ventriloquism, so that *The Eighty-Minute Hour* tells itself as an onomatopoeia of selfhood, an elbowing doubletake of the author to the effect: Well I guess *that's* the sound I make, right guys?: but without admitting it, except in Julliann's moment of melancholia output whose confession I don't find to bear convincingly tidings, frankly.

Sure. At some level *any* book's plot and characters are nothing more than superfetations of its voice, onomatopoeia, and Mr Aldiss *pur* may well have intended to hang his spoofing of space opera conventions onto a travesty of the Session Fallacy so common to science fiction as a whole; but to follow that line of thought begs the question of what the book itself says and *does* to one, and succumbs to another Fallacy — The Intentional. No. *The Eighty-Minute Hour* fails precisely because its plot and characters, however intended to be read under a claim of derisive spoofing, are superfetations of the wrong voice.

There is a story.

After a devastating war, Earth's surviving nations have grouped themselves into two opposing blocs, the larger of which Attica Saigon Smix dominates; but where is Attica Saigon Smix? Projections of this gentleman stalk the earth and chair conferences, but the real Attica Saigon Smix has used his scientists' discoveries to create a hideaway for himself deep within an alternate phase of reality, an "ecopicosystem" whose matrix lies within a pendant he has given to Monty Zoomer *but* Monty Zoomer has ignorantly passed it on, causing a lot of toing and froing, most of which is inexplicable at first as the *role of the pendant* only achieves the extremely muddy focus it eventually attains very very late in the book, deeper than plummet sounds. The smaller bloc of nations features the gormless Surinat clan, which includes the legless dreamer of Julliann's trek into the Dread Brain Mist and the legless narrator as well, who is so transparent to the self-preening voice of the book we tend to forget him. Between the two factious blocs, and insidiously coming to control both of them, we find the computer complex, whose own Dickian projection, Thunderbird Smith, both shouts a lot and does manage to elicit some effective imagery, here and there. Conspiring to an autotelic dominance of mankind (as in all genre vulgarizations of Jacques Ellul and Mumford, who have already done their formidable best to map the peripheralization of humanity in a world of technical solutions, a Conspiracy must be adduced) the Computer Complex (to render caps unto Caesar) devises the eighty-minute hour, apparently as a morale-breaker, and is eagerly on the look-out for Attica Saigon Smix's hideaway, so as to control him too; and on this, and on the pendant, and on the intrusion of certain time-turbulences, the plot turns.

These turbulences whisk — like an author's eraser — various protagonists off the scene into the deep past or future, causing the Computer Complex to chase the pendant "containing" the Smix ecopicosystem billions of years backwards through time, eventually to land for a confrontation scene on the old fifth planet, which soon explodes — like an overheated eraser — only to become the asteroid belt. But an element of the Computer Complex has survived the explosion, and retains possession of the pendant, which it deposits on Mars to be discovered, much much later, by the evil Dr Chaplain whose eros control device (modelled on the hypothalamus) itself turns out to have been utilized by the Complex in the deep past as a model for the hypothalamus in its (the Complex's) godlike engineering back then of the homeostatic phyla, making homo sapiens possible in the first place. Before the novel begins, Chaplain has sold the pendant to Attica Saigon Smix ....

But what the hell's the use? So what if there's a plot, a sort of contortuplication high that even the scantiest synopsis almost rescues by revoicing it? So what if characters abound? By merely naming them, synopsis gives them a more abundant life, if only potentially, than ever the voice of *The Eighty-Minute Hour* would dream of permitting in its shape. To rescue plot or to name characters from that benumbing pazzazz falls into one of the traps it sets for the reader — that of believing anything in the book except the sound of its telling. Terminally the implied author utters through his ghostly puppets a buffo vaudeville — "Think! Take us with you wherever you wend, / Else our Hour of Existence is now at an end, / So think, think, think, again!" — and suddenly there came over me a vision of the dear Mr Barrie bullying helpless children from his guise of Tinkerbell. And suddenly I knew the shape of my animus against the implied Mr Aldiss of this book. Even as a child I always longed to stomp Tinkerbell.

New Worlds Quarterly 8//1975

15//NW4//Farmer/Niven/Harrison/Clarke:

Birdseed for Our Feathered Fans

Chorusing panjandra in falsetto shill the reader on his rounds: Buy me! Buy me! They laughed when I sat down at the typewriter, but now I'm Larry Niven! They kicked sand in my face (reminisces Philip José Farmer) but now I'm erect. Wham bam (adds Harry Harrison) bam bam bam bam bam.

Particularly biodegradable in this new lot, like Chinese food, is Mr Farmer's latest ware, *Traitor to the Living* (Ballantine, 1974), which shuffles through several of his abiding concerns rather faster than the eye can see, and the novel certainly gives the impression of having been written faster than its author could type.

"Gordon Carfax moaned," it begins, but what he's moaning about (his dead wife) is soon forgotten, along with a variety of other establishing data, like the mystery of his earlier nervous breakdown, and a previous wife, and numerous other hints and half-hints to the reader that Carfax (like most Farmer heroes of late, and like almost any science fiction protagonist you could name who happens to boast an impaired memory) is in fact immortal, or Tarzan, or Christ, or a super-criminal from Andromeda whose sin was his decision to bring fire to the natives (and a light to Stanley Kubrick's Menippean eye), but please, sir, please, not just a lousy ex-private-eye, Mr Farmer, anything but that.

— Aw shaddup, litcrit poof. Like get carried away on the flood of narrative, like.

So it's sink or swim: Gordon Carfax (ex-lousy-private-eye and now Professor of Medieval History, his appointment to this post being yet another story we're not quite told) has challenged Raymond Western's claim to have found out what happens after death through a computer link called MEDIUM (though what that's an acronym for I seem to have missed); once posthumous, dead folk become *sembs* (a form of "energy"), in which form they do nothing more than circle around one another interminably, "in very complicated but limited and repetitive orbits, " according to Western. No way, counters Professor Carfax — *sembs* are in fact nothing but unfriendly aliens *imitating* the dead for their own purposes. Beware! Beware! At this point the novel seems about ready to build itself into a narrative dramatizing the conflict between these two views, but in fact the nitwit Professor's idea is so ludicrously unworkable that Mr Farmer allows him to drop it (behind the reader's back) while other things are happening stage-front, like for instance the edgy affair between Carfax and his cousin Elizabeth, who claims that Western stole MEDIUM from her father, Carfax's uncle, and (for good measure) murdered him as well, all of which motivates the good Professor of Medieval History and ex-private-eye to confront his suave but villainous adversary with these harsh accusations pronto. But Western (in fact the apparent Western is *actually* a *semb* who was formerly James Fisk [1834-1872], the Barnum of Wall Street) immediately changes bodies via MEDIUM with Elizabeth, after a Ringling Brothers' worth of needless stock adventure shticks which comprise the bulk of the novel. Elizabeth (Raymond [*semb* {James Fisk}] Western) then fucks Professor Carfax, only postcoitally to reveal to the bemused ex-private-eye his/her nefarious plans for dealing with all Carfaxes, not excluding the dead uncle (Elizabeth's Dad) who has until now been completely forgotten, even though he's a *semb* in a particularly boring orbit and eager to have a chat. He/she then dumps the extremely inept ex-private-eye, possibly in a state of shock from having fucked the Barnum of Wall Street, into the bowels of MEDIUM which transliterates him to the *semb* universe (or — more precisely, for Farmer is nothing but precise about data he intends to drop — to the *embu*) and then right out of it again, into the body of a luscious female whose bare breasts the unemployable shamus had once eyed lustfully (presumably her human soul becomes a *semb* in *embu* limbo, which is a sorry fate, but if Farmer doesn't care why should we): and now they're *his* breasts: and he can make them *heave*: and he (the dick with tits) asks for a phone so he can tell the enormously tall red-haired Senator (just never mind how *he* gets into the story) all about James Fisk and his psychotic plan to transform all Carfaxes into *sembs* and also to demolish the world with energy exchanges: and the novel ends with a clunk, possibly at the exact number of words it was contracted for.

What this piece of dizzy bumph most clearly conveys to the reader sufficiently hornswoggled to complete it is a sense of dropped stitches, dropped themes, dropped tropes, and even the Dropped Unnamable, because sex isn't very much fun either. It's a dangerously shoddy piece of merchandise for Mr Farmer to hawk, and adulterates his brand: for after all, it's only because he can do so very much better that one spends so much time (first) reading *Traitor to the Living*, (second) trying to believe one's eyes, and only (third) dropping it.

Larry Niven — the one with the fixed grin — fills his stall once again with a story from the sequence *Ringworld* was supposed to end, or so he's told us, and though *Protector* (Ballantine, 1974) isn't half-bad, by now he's stuffed his series with so many irreconcilable aliens and gadgets and denouements that this effort (especially as it comes early in the chronology that leads to *Ringworld*) nearly shakes the whole sequence to little bits. Most future historians are properly conservative of their material, and distinctly tend to avoid writing the kind of story whose basic premise would fundamentally restructure the universe it is supposed — one might think — to add a brick or buttress to. Mr Niven's trouble seems to be a kind of Can-Do optimism about the amount of torsion he can apply to a future history without turning it into confetti.

Take *Protector*, whose initial protagonist is a sample — from a long ways away across the galaxy — of the long-lost adult form of homo sapiens, and who has come to Sol to take care of an abandoned colony of adolescent Breeders, which is us. Necessary for change-over to adult form is a kind of yam that won't grow on Earth: but the Protector soon feeds some from his private hoard to a Breeder named Brennan, who soon realizes that more Protectors are on their way from the home system, because according to their version of how to protect their own Breeders they must make war to the death against homo sapiens, who have mutated slightly. Brennan immediately hightails it to Home, a planet established in an earlier volume of the series, and prepares to transform it (dictatorially, as usual in space opera) in preparation for the coming war.

All of which is enjoyable enough, though a structural caesura in the middle of it is sadly mismanaged: but just where do these revelations about homo sapiens and transformations of future history leave Mr Niven's other books? I wouldn't know. I couldn't work it out.

After Harry Harrison's lousy *Stainless Steel Rat's Revenge*, it's a pleasure to note that *The Stainless Steel Rat Saves the World* (Faber, 1974) comes a long way back toward the form of the first book in the series, fifteen years old now, *The Stainless Steel Rat*, and a joy forever. If the current offering stops short of a full return to the level of that book, it's because Mr Harrison insists on underlining, with a corrosive jokiness, the kinetic rataplan he puts his hero through; and the last thing this sort of adventure needs is wisecracks to eat away at the suspension of disbelief.

(A note for serious students: to chart the decay and partial recovery of the Rat sequence, trace the decline of the first book's formidable Inskipp into a pop-eyed gildersleeve fit for a Retief scam in the second, and his virtual elimination in the third. It's something of a cheap trick on Inskipp, Mr Harrison.)

The story involves time travel and is therefore untellable.

New Worlds Quarterly 7//1974

The Clone of Arthur C Clarke

Once upon a time, long ago in the exciting 60s, darkbearded saturnine fatfaced Stanley Kubrick happened to read a story by the engaging bespectacled Arthur C Clarke, then as now a Senior Dean of our own sf. The story, which was called "The Sentinel," inspired in Stanley Kubrick some extremely ambitious and worldly thoughts. If only I could get Arthur's permission on the dotted line, I could very nearly (thought Stanley Kubrick) laugh Western civilisation to death with *a movie version*. Later that night in Ceylon Mr Clarke, one of the colossi of our own sf, awoke from fretful slumber to find standing over his bed a darkbearded saturnine fatfaced Mephistophelean figure clutching a copy of "The Sentinel" in pallid early-Yeatsian hands.

— Good evening, Arthur, said Stanley (for it was he). I want to offer you the world. You only have to sign here.

He thrust a contract forward, and the knife.

— Offer me the world? said Arthur, rightly skeptical but obscurely attracted to the plump charismatic leprechaun-like figure by his bed. Silly boy, he said. I *already* love the world and all its intricate doings, and it is enough for me that I can be happy explaining the workings of the world to all my friends. Here, look at this transparent plastic man with all his nerves and organs showing, which I keep by my writing desk for easy reference. He's my friend, Stanley. What a piece of work is a man! You can see that in his hand he holds a copy of *Men Like Gods* by H G Wells. "The jewel on the reptile's head that had brought Utopia out of the confusions of human life," says H G Wells in that very book, Stanley, "was curiosity, the play impulse, prolonged and expanded in adult life into an insatiable appetite for knowledge and an habitual creative agency. All Utopians had become as little children, learners and makers." So let that be my answer, Stanley, H G's and mine. I am as a child, and I play with my transparent man. Like a jewel, he glows. What need have I for riches?

— Christ Arthur that was moving, expostulated the insistent, mesmeric Stanley. But lend me an ear for just a moment, will ya guy? Arthur, friend, teacher, did you know you're a kind of guru to me, Arthur? No kidden. Last week I was chewing the fat with one of the Washington consiglieri, he was showing some signs of metal fatigue, rational-hope-for-the-future-wise you know? So I mention your name as a man of hope, guy, and he says: Stanley my boy, would that Arthur C Clarke were with me at this very moment to guide me as I face the problems of burgeoning technology, not to speak of the death of Lake Erie, nor of the return-of-psychopathic-vets-from-Nam-perplex, and so forth. Art guy, don't it start to penetrate? We need guidance, Art. Come an be our guru, guy. Point us in the direction of tomorrow. We're all stuck down here in the cesspool without ya.

— "Cesspool," Stanley? chided the redoubtable sf writer. As guests here in balmy Ceylon, we tend to eschew language like that.

— Just a figure of speech, smiled the sinister *auteur terrible*, crossing his fingers behind his back. But alla same, don't it kinda show what a lousy mess we're in, when words like Shitsville and cesspool and abattoir and nada nada come so easy to the lips of cultural apex hitmen like moi? You gotta help us, Art. You gotta show us the high-road outta Shitsville where it sometimes looks like we're highballing into the big dark like, you know, like maybe we shoulda deepsixed Newton and all those other sleepwalker fruitcakes back when before they had a chance to dump us into Shitsville, Art, where the centre don't hold, and you sleep rough and your lungs rot and you get warts offa the kindly zephyr from the chemical plant here in Shitsville, baby. O my God, Art, the strain, the anguish. It's like Rectumsville down here baby. It's the hole in the bottom of the sink. It's Lake Erie.

— Hush, soothed the sf colossus, deeply moved by the squat mogul's plight, hush now. Don't worry about a thing. Everything is going to be all right now, you've just been having a bad dream. Here, let me tell you something. I'm going to write you a *nice* script about the new dawn. It may *just* help to save this dear world of ours, Stanley. And Arthur C Clarke took the triplicate form, and the knife, and signed the form with his pricked finger, and dropped back to sleep thinking, What a good boy am I to merit such a treat.

But Stanley had other thoughts as he buzzed back into the dark post-industrial West. So it's a dear sweet worldums, Arthur, is it (he thought), and it's peopled with nice transparent plastic men who like the future, is it? Arthur, do you know what I'm going to do? I'm going to take the script you give me, and out of the bland technological optimism it will reek of I'm going to make *2001, A Space Odyssey*. Ha ha ha. Where the heroes you write for me will be makers and doers transparent to the light of reason within them which defines their natures, mine will be stale hollow puppets, bleached-out victims of the technology or special effects *your* heroes integrate with smiling. Where the story you'll write will model the *connectedness* of things and the clear entailments of reason as it calls the tune of the deep-structure of the world, my story will plummet sickeningly into a caesura between the discovery of the fathomless rectangle on the Moon and the Jupiter mission that inexplicably follows. Where your superman will "think" of something to do with himself, mine will only stare through us hairy mortals chillingly, as *I* try to do in *my* art. Arthur, I will take your script and will hardly change a word. I won't need to. Just a sign-change here, a semiotic nudge there, an overlit dead muffled interminable silence between the lines, Arthur, and everyone will be able to see that beneath your dream of immanent reason squats Shitsville, where we live.

And he did.

And Arthur gazed — possibly in bewilderment — at what Stanley had done to his daydreams of enhancement, and wrote a novelization of *2001* full of connectedness and transparency and good-will, though no one seemed to listen, so then he wrote *Rendezvous with Rama* (1973), chockful of c and t and g-w, and won awards and kudos, and now he's done it again, published another novel, *Imperial Earth* (Gollancz, 1975), redolent of the very same sustaining value-system, so that the moral of the fable of the midnight gabfest of Stanley and Arthur still holds true: Do not sell your dreams of c and t and g-w to the devil, for he will know what to do with them.

Imperial Earth could not be called a good novel, but to dismiss it as a failed fiction — because its characters are cardboard, its storyline exiguous, and so forth — would be to deny by omission the translucent, effortless ephiphanousness of the book, which resides less in its nature as a novel than in the fact that it reads as a kind of elated *prophecy* of a time to come beyond our time of troubles when population will be controlled, conflicts among nations stilled, sexual dimorphism soothed of those rough edges and coulisses we all skirt these days, and the world itself — the green Earth — will have been returned to its natural state. Men Like Gods Ville.

Duncan Makenzie is a third generation clone, grandson and son of the Chief Executives of Titan, Saturn's vast moon. He experiences no traumas at being identikit; his relations with Pop and Grandpop Clone benignly reverse the scarifying descent into age of the protagonist at the end of *2001* [and it might be noted that Gene Wolfe's *The Fifth Head of Cerberus*, which takes a radically darker view of the imprisoning implications of being cloned by a supremo Dad, was published just a few years earlier *1986*]. Duncan knows where his next meal is coming from, as Titan prospers immensely by supplying the inner planets with hydrogen to fuel commerce. Invited to visit Earth to help celebrate the 500th anniversary of the American Revolution, Duncan accepts the chance to tumble down the gravity well with clear-skinned boyish enthusiasm; in any case, it's time for him to go to Earth to clone off a fourth Makenzie. Only fly in the ointment is Duncan's childhood pal, the brilliant but unbalanced Karl, a blond Adonis and creative research scientist who envies Duncan because he's a Makenzie.

Duncan flies to Earth; Duncan sees what Earth is like in 2276, and like any protagonist in a juvenile (though he's past 30), he is sort of gee-whizzed by the joy of things. Later Karl dies in pathetic circumstances, and Duncan clones his corpse and returns to Titan with a blond baby, to upset the apple cart *just a little*. So not very much happens. The book's heart lies in its lengthy, exhilarated descriptions of the flight to Earth and of Duncan's expanding perceptions once he gets there. *Imperial Earth* is a travelogue of the kind of future Arthur C Clarke may well actually believe we're going to get. The effect is soothing, pathos-ridden, uplifting; a sort of pastoral high. The occasional sombre note no more turns Clarke into Barry Malzberg than "Recessional" turned Kipling into George Gissing.

Filmed, *Imperial Earth* would be a vision of decerebrate zombies roaming Alphaville. So what is truth? Turn away, do not wait for the answer. Maybe we don't really need the bloody movie.

New Worlds Quarterly 10//1976

16//NW5:

Trope Exposure

Gaw. Here I have opened my mouth to gape in the dark at the silver screen, which is about to hallucinate me on request and to strobe my privacy on request with a science fiction movie made in 1954 on time-honoured generic lines, when suddenly I find myself ingesting cigarette smoke exuded from the disgusting lungs of the city slickers in the audience who disease us with their habit in places where humans congregate and all must breathe, but that's life. Life is a fascist state with its prick up and the hands of Esau, a conspiracy of role moles against entropy; the habits and the haecceity or *thingness* of others constantly forces you to pass for being alive: forces you into arrant impostures to keep the dogs off, dissolution off. The cigarette smoke of others is what you might call an example of closet entropy, entropy camouflaged as a trope (or vector) of the role of addicted human. Heat death in drag, that's life. Yuck yuck yuck, they'll say, if you accuse them of invading your privacy with their poisonous vectors, these humans addicted to themselves, chuckling with the self-indulgence that signals a connivance claim on those they victimize, as what genre doesn't: yuck I guess the habit's got me yuck I've given up smoking a hundred times yuck.

So life is boundary maintenance against the enemy's story, so I close my mouth. The film begins. Life and art — at any rate, life and the science fiction film made in 1954 on time-honoured generic lines — differ in that the incursion of the latter is solicited. Like docked triffids in imaginary gardens, the generic film is safer than life in other ways, too, as we've always known (though I do remember watching Bob Hope in *Paleface* when it came out and wondering at the hugeness of a movie theatre that could hold so much desert). In the absence of Sensurround, which makes you want to go toidy, a genre product's ontological locale is safely anaesthetized as "existing" *prior* to the signs it comprises on the screen of an enactment completed into a shape you can blame: because even while you're pretending to be hallucinated you can *remember* what's going to happen. Which is not the case, or should not be the case, in non-generic work, whose ontological locale is at least rhetorically simultaneous to its enactment. Non-generic art makes the large claim to ordonnate something of the intolerable and chaotic presentness of life itself, with its billion balkanized extras and no auteur, its demand on us lifers that we maintain a constant wariness in the mind's eye, that we maintain a capacity to predict and channel the intrusions of other extras, to shift genres like a cardsharp. Like moles in the rotten state.

For their audiences, generic productions can be perceived as mnemonic plays upon an anaesthetized matrix; this matrix — this associative net of expectations or trammels—comprises plot segments, character icons, Production Code opacities, visual syntax, sexual skews, segmented tropes, channelled tropes, blocked tropes, and everything perceived of as typically existing *prior to* the work watched, in the vast affinity of previous works defined as making up or contributing to the particular genre or subgenre in question. In referring to matrices of this sort, *Them*, for instance, a science fiction film made in 1954 on time-honoured generic lines which I am about to return to for the first time, presents itself, in other words, as a form of rhetoric. The arguments thus carried — however seemingly coherent — are logically dependent on the fact that rhetoric itself lays on a presupposition of the accessibility of the world to the forms of "argument" that comprise it, to the vast affinity of the prior. If rhetoric is a kind of *passacaglia*, then the world (the individual work) must be transparent to the entailments of the tune. Any other forms of truth — any dissonant notes the audience can register, like casting the wrong actor in the role of duplicitous father figure, who in American films is the one with the habit of making cognitive speculations about the nature of social realities, which means he has a sense of wonder, which means he is a subversive — tend to fog the plate, so that the film tends to become indecipherable, untrue to the network of precedents, and begins to threaten the reader, just as life does, outside the play dark. Generic works are devices for casting back, not neologisms to greet the world afresh. In the true novel, whose existence is posited frequently enough, there can be no mnemonic play: but of course the true novel, if written, could not be understood, any more than Semele could truly understand Apollo as he fucked her to death.

In a TLS review (28 February 1975), Niko Tinbergen suggests that "the motivating systems ... involved in religious behaviour" might include

> a fusion of a number of "natural" deep-rooted response systems, such as our submissive attitude to people whom we admire and respect; our limited but real social co-operativeness; our need for feeling at home in familiar surroundings; our fear of threatening agents even within this familiar "home range" [or genre]; and our resigned acceptance of the incomprehensibility of our world.

But it is a world whose organized religions play at jingle bells in Flanders Fields, still swank but rotting, like lepers in Santa Claus gear. We no longer live in a world we can perceive as transparent to the doggerel rhetorics of an established Church; generically, the Church reached the end of its tether a long while ago. Perhaps (it is not an original thought) the proliferation of generic literatures during the course of this century, along with a similar breeding of "new paradigm" cults and sects, can be read as symptomatic of the sort of needs or "response systems" Professor Tinbergen adduces, "God" help us. If so, the Summa Theologicae of the twentieth century will be a properly comprehensive encyclopedia of the Hollywood trope, whose star avatars abide in the seventh heaven.

Penetrating the contaminating cigarette smoke of the barbarians with stirrups who ceaselessly besiege the frontier encampments of our lives, *Them* really does begin, with an aerial view of the American desert, a shot whose import is immediately transparent to the viewer: because it is the desert in 1954, we know it's very likely that Them, whatever they turn out to be, will have something to do with nuclear explosions; because we are in a moving plane, we know that something has probably already happened, and that director Gordon Douglas (no auteur but crafty) has plumped us in medias res, as the sight of a police car bucking with speed and of a darling small girl wandering traumatized across the cactusy burning sands soon confirms. So it goes. Of the two officers in the speeding car, one is a nobody who will consequently, by definition, soon fall victim to Them, and the other is played by James Whitmore, whose presence carries a semiotic burden — a mnemonic *move* — from the matrix in which "James Whitmore" is an axon of sorts. As established in *The Asphalt Jungle* (1950), "James Whitmore" signs onto our retinas as craggy, sincere, mulish, sentimental, dumb, prone to pair-bonding with other males, though very much a family man, and kind of religious; in short, a loser. We remember these attributes and apply them instanter to the cop in the car in *Them.* We "remember" that he is a straight cop, mulish, prone to pair-bonding with his doomed buddy, and sentimentally familiar in his responses to the darling girl who has been traumatized — as it had to be — by the death of her parents, killed by Them. A few sequences later, when Them exterminate his buddy, we also "remember" that "James Whitmore" will surely give up his life somewhere near the end of the film (and two-thirds of the way through, we'll be able to recognize a false resolution to the crisis created by Them through his continuance among the living) both to avenge the death of his pair-bond, and to save either the little girl herself (who might be retained in the film for that purpose) or possibly some substitute (another little girl, perhaps, or maybe a nun). Just how "James Whitmore" is fated to die doesn't much matter; what's important in the sign language of genre is that from the beginning of the film we (and by we I mean most of the audience) know that "James Whitmore" is a goner for sure, and that we have not yet met the actual protagonist of *Them*, because protagonists in science fiction films in 1954 cannot be *losers.*

Heroes survive, and so does America.

But a simplified adducing of cues like this can only begin to plumb the depths of our knowledge of why "James Whitmore" cannot be the protagonist of *Them.* How we know (or remember) that he is ontologically a second lead, a character part; how we know he has too much "character" to be anything *but* a loser or earth; how we know that heroes in 1954 do not pair-bond; how we know that police officers are too mundane to spearhead a film about nuclear disasters: the sources and routes to the conscious mind of these forms of knowledge would require many viewings of the film in question to even begin to understand, and hair-raisingly interminable exposition (a thousand words per frame) to even begin to make clear. But we *do* know, and our shared awareness of a structural retard — the delay in introducing the hero — comprises part of the pleasure of our viewing.

The retard will not be resolved until the appearance some time on of James Arness as an FBI investigator, whose plenipotentiary potency is significantly heralded through his arrival by plane. In 1954, James Arness has no character at all, for *Gunsmoke* has not yet begun to control the meaning of his presence; the director *positions* him into the role of protagonist, enhaloes him with protagony vibes, so that by the time the scientist's daughter tumbles out of the potent plane we know that James Arness will win the battle against whatever unnatural phenomenon Them represent because of his instant love for her and certain other cues. So it goes. There are some turns we won't be able to anticipate until the actor who represents the film's "choice" of moves makes his appearance out of the matrix, or well of being. Is the scientist in the film going to be evil (that is, creative) or will he be benevolent (that is, an expert)? Not until Edmund Gwenn appears, and we can see that he is *twinkling*, can we know that in this movie the scientist will be on the side of the guys in the government, and that, as a direct consequence, the origin of Them will be ascribed to the unknown effects of atomic radiation, and not to the Weltschmerz of a hypomanic bookworm with dandruff and an unquenchable lust for worldly power (that is, a research scientist) experimenting in things men were not meant to know. In *Them*, Edmund Gwenn (that is, the Stars and Stripes) is *meant* to know. Them, incidentally, turn out to be giant mutated ants who eat people. In the false resolution their desert nest is fumigated (though not "James Whitmore"). In the final sequence, the last of the migratory queens (plus one craggy pair-bonder, who does manage to save the children) are given to the flames in the storm sewers beneath the streets of Los Angeles, the very same sewers that seem to be about to erupt with giant ants in *Point Blank* (1967) but don't.

Most of the generic moves visible in *Them*, and it should be kept in mind that there are literally thousands of them, will have been recognized by most viewers of the film, who will have counted on this sort of high profile genericness for much of their pleasure. Indeed, an intense visibility of moves, or trope exposure, does arguably distinguish not only the generic film but maybe cinema as a whole from other narrative arts. Industrial, sociological, historical and ontological reasons for this —as well as obvious ones about the sensorium film addresses — can be brought forward by the film critic, most of whose groundwork is still to be done. At this early date, two of his primary tasks must still be the creation of an adequate working distinction of film from the other arts, and the amassing of a vocabulary of those double-tense visual verbs we simplify by calling them *moves*. Films work through a rhetoric that claims (perhaps not falsely) to bare and simultaneously to soothe the memoriousness of perception, so our eyes pun flowing with tears. Gratefully we can play with ourselves in safety, in the dark, with the corsets of our drag unlaced a little, because these risen dreams we plug into, though stroboscopic, do not break the film of the past.

New Worlds Quarterly 9//1975

17//Aces//Swanwick/Shepard/Gibson:

1/Michael Swanwick

Promises, promises. The new series of Ace Specials is promising. Terry Carr, who edited the first series of Ace Specials too, back in the 1960s when so few books were being published you could read them, is promising. He is promising us a good read. "If you're getting a little tired of reading science fiction novels that are just like the ones you read last month or last year," he promises, "this book is for you." But I give you my word: if you're getting a little tired of reading introductions that are just like the ones you read last month or last year, don't read most of Mr Carr's introduction to *In the Drift* (Ace Special, 1985), because most of Mr Carr's introduction to *In the Drift* is the very same introduction that prefaces with the very same promises the first five books — *The Wild Shore* by Kim Stanley Robinson, *Green Eyes* by Lucius Shepard, *Neuromancer* by William Gibson, *Palimpsests* by Carter Scholz and Glenn Harcourt, and *Them Bones* by Howard Waldrop — mostly. And Michael Swanwick is promising.

He has also fixed us up. *In the Drift* is far too well written, and far too cagey in its avoidance of any excess expenditure of creative energy, to mislead the wary reviewer — on his managing, dizzy and dejected and done, to finish the thing — into making a charge of incompetence. The retreat of *In the Drift* from the novelistic coulisses of its opening section is nothing but professional, nor in any way does Mr Swanwick show himself to be outstretched or flummoxed by the challenges of that opening section, whose protagonist he ably puts through a shattering *rite de passage* into an adulthood poisoned (in a chancy but successful zeugma) by guilt and radiation, for the America Piotrowicz inhabits has disintegrated after a nuclear accident at (odd choice: does Mr Swanwick intend positing an alternate universe here?) Three Mile Island. Originally published as "Mummer Kiss" in 1981, these first 57 pages of *In the Drift* seem to promise, along with the de rigeur rhodomontade of genre action, something of a dialectical expansion of the terms of that zeugma.

But nothing of the sort happens. It may be because *In the Drift* is a fixup, which we can define (once again) as (usually) a series of previously written stories patched together by newly composed interstitial material, or maybe just the previously written stories all alone. These stories will have originally been written with a fixup in view, or maybe not. Sometimes the stories — *In the Drift* for instance also includes a couple of previously unpublished segments plus "Marrow Death" from 1984 — will be asked to mate into something like a narrative sequence, as happens here, one usually extending over a considerable time span, as happens here, and without any continuity of point of view: and sure enough, we soon lose sight of Piotrowicz, except through the eyes of others, who catch intermittent glimpses of a template soldier on horseback weathering badly. And the further we are taken from Piotrowicz, the dumber this book gets, because Piotrowicz's complex angular mind is the only rounded human consciousness Mr Swanwick has cared to create in this text. Deftly and professionally he retreats, as the novel he has assembled slithers onward, into that termitarium of American sf kitsch where paranormal powers and a decayed populism miscegenate dimly to beget a new religion that will transform the lives of the oppressed (they do *imagine* these things so easily in America), and the disjointed congeries of story-wedges he uses to "convey" his sham epic is no more than a labour-saving device, the kind of dodge or abdication for which the fixup form might almost have been invented specifically to accommodate, so readily does its question-begging structure camouflage failures of cohesion and follow-through. Given the temptations of the form, given the fact that it is very difficult to write a good fixup and terribly easy to write a lousy one, Mr Swanwick should have written a novel instead.

There is nothing intrinsically *wrong* with the disjointedness of narrative flow, or with the slackness in the chain/web of narrative causality, that seem inherent in any text constructed as a fixup; indeed, sagaciously transfigured, the fixup might be seen as a modernist recapture of the episodic chronicles that comprise one of the strands leading to the modern novel, and hence as a subversion of conventional narrative. Fat chance, generally. Most fixups exhibit a narrative structure one might call *bugger's epic*. The reader of the usual fixup is like a gumshoe bugging a conference, or taping the private life of a hero whose inner concerns he cannot get a bead on. The vision he gets of the world of the text whose peepholes he's glued to will be fragmented, highlit, stroboscopic, rather dizzying (Van Vogt Yaw), oddly demeaning and deeply frustrating. The wrong people will be standing too close to the mike, gossiping of Michelangelo. The telephoto closeup of the moment *directly preceding* the assassination will give the gumshoe an empty feeling inside. Somewhere out of sight of our poor bugger (he is us), anonymous adults (like Keith Piotrowicz) will be doing the difficult things it might take work to envisage, determining the shape of the next hundred years of post-catastrophe America while the foreground is choked up with the peregrinations of extras (*In the Drift* boasts *two* healer/precog Joans of Arc, only one of whom actually gets burned alive). All the same, back at his peephole, doing Mr Swanwick's work for him, insecurely, humbly, tenaciously, the faithful reader (he's a poor bugger) will begin to perceive with all his might the lineaments of an epic, for he will have been constructing, out of the salad of orts he's been given to digest, that larger story which the author has not bothered to write. Just precisely because there *are* absences at the heart of the fixup, that reader will populate those absences with signs and portents of epic narrativity which the text has not earned, merely *warranted*. Because Nature abhors a vacuum; because a hectic semiosis webs all absences with vistas and denizens. It is the rage for order. And in any case, if a fixup text is *not* intended to represent selections from a larger story, then why has it been constructed as a fixup in the first place? If there is a pliant seamless tale to be told, a narrative couchable as one sustained slur of continuity, even though that sleight-of-hand last the length of the novel, then there can be no aesthetic sanction for opening yaws of uncouched absence between disjunct sections. To do so is to claim that individual sections mean not only what they say, but that they also point to a larger shape they highlight. In a bad fixup (like *In the Drift*) that larger shape will be illuminated by little more than the patchwork quilt of clichés of outward regard that any sf reader can (and must, poor bugger) create out of the generic protocols he/she's memorized over the years. [See the previous chapter, "Trope Exposure " *1986*.] Mr Swanwick need merely point yawning. In the "true" fixup, that interrogates our fixed generic vision, a succession of estranging absences can serve to subvert us, to clear our minds of that slur of continuity by which mimetic romance spiels stabilize the world, and anaesthetize our reading of the world, so that, in the fixity of the perceived world, we founder. Indeed, at the end of this century of eliding glare, it may well be the case that no epic can be spoken without cooptation, nor incanted, nor tolled: for that which can be spoken is already Coca Cola.

So it is of our condition to make some sense out of *In the Drift*, in the absence of Mr Swanwick. As his ravaged Philadelphia suffers no enriching sea-change after Piotrowicz reaches adulthood, because the author has left both Philadelphia and Piotrowicz in the lurch, it's us poor buggers who are forced to construct, out of our readings of dozens of post-catastrophe American sf writers and M John Harrison (sleazy Brit) too, a theatre of ghost protocols that serves somehow to keep alive the mummers and mutants of the gaudy urban heartwood Mr Swanwick gestured at, to enact (out of absence) the self-destructive contortions of the Philadelphia godfathers as they try to keep their city "safe" from any awareness that it, too, lies within the Drift-Zone where the radiation count precludes normal lifespans, normal breeding. The releasing protocols for this bugger's epic haunt the dense pages of "Mummer Kiss," and it did seem that the interactions between Keith Piotrowicz and his city might well grow — as the book progressed — into a mature tragedy. But no.

No. Off we go on page 58 to the post-catastrophe Greenwood, all Ernst-and-water, there to meet a vampire precog named Sam, who will turn out to be the first of the Joans, along with a gruff but kindhearted dwarf physician who keeps her supplied with animal blood. We meet other mutants. They are depressed and ignorant. Piotrowicz extends his penis sufficiently far into the text to beget Joan of Arc Two on Joan of Arc One, and disappears again, like a diorama humour. Joan Two is even more "talented" than her mother, who is now dead, but whose ghost does encore cute for a while. Through her paranormal wisdom, she realizes that the benighted locals, caught between the real and complex concerns of warring city states (fill in the blanks), need *a new religion*, preferably one consistent with a revolutionary consciousness (maybe like the religion of Jesus before the Christians got to it). Dying of radiation in any case, she blackmails Piotrowicz (now an old man) into burning her at the stake. She reckons this will catalyze (rather than merely heat) the masses, and that they will then prevail. Whether or not the masses are in fact catalyzed we do not discover, as the book ends at this point, where it might have gotten difficult to write. And that's the ball game. Mr Swanwick, a grown man, a clever writer, a knowing craftsman, must know damn well what he hasn't accomplished in this dereliction of a book. And what he has not accomplished will not live on after him.

Foundation 33//Spring 1985

2/Lucius Shepard

Because of the inchoate profusion of idea and anecdote which chokes it half to death, and because its plot sets a plethora of hares into motion every which way like hares will, Lucius Shepard's first novel, *Green Eyes* (Ace Special, 1984), must be adjudged something of a failure, for the book adds up to considerably less than the sum of its parts. Taken in judicious doses, however, those parts are quite extraordinary, and Shepard's use of voodoo themes says something of real interest about the current state of sophistication of the science fiction genre in the United States.

In the near future of America, a privately financed research organization, housed in the Deep South, has succeeded in creating laboratory zombies. By injecting bacteria from a chosen graveyard into recently dead cadavers, Doctors Ezawa and Edman have managed to install new personalities in the undead. These personalities seem to concentrate in themselves certain paradigmatic aspects of what it means to be human. Some are evil, some frenetic; one is a scientist, another — the protagonist — a dark poet. All are mesmeric, all are hauntingly regal, as though they were deep archetypes reborn. And indeed they are exactly that.

It is when Donnell Harrison, the Luciferian poet, escapes the institute and goes to ground in bayou country that the novel begins to split into its parts. Shepard may know the lay of the land and the accents of its gothic inhabitants, but much of this territory is familiar to any reader of Southern American fiction; the raw impasto of Shepard's local-colourist canvas simply gums up the works of his story. With his institute girl-friend, Donnell now tries to find a cure for the fatal proliferation of the bacteria, which have given him life and selfhood only to overbreed fatally, causing his eyes to turn green. Being able to read electromagnetic vibrations, he also cures the sick. He also attends a revival meeting and breaks it up in a fit of hypnotic iconoclasm. And so on.

Finally Donnell and the faithful lissome Jocundra become embroiled with the half-insane descendant of a long-dead voodoo apparatchik who helps him build a *veve* — an occult focusing device made of copper — through which he controls the bacteria, travels to a harsh fantasy land, all the while becoming more and more akin to the *gros bon ange*, or primordial soul, of an entity of the voodoo pantheon. He destroys some of those who would use voodoo for ill; finds out that the institute has been itself implicated in voodoo; and dies, or finds transcendental rebirth in the analogue land of true dreams.

It is, of course, all too much. What remains is humid patches of local colour, some oddly effective poetry, the fragments of a genuinely interesting exploration of biological engineering and mind-states, and the sense that there is, at least for American science fiction writers, something inherently useful in the concept of voodoo. By now it is a truism that the science fiction genre houses a strong and sometimes desperate urgency to transcend this mortal coil and go travelling. Unlike most religions, or movements tinged with some religious aspect, voodoo is intensely pragmatic. It is a religion for those — most were originally slaves — who have to cope with an almost intolerable environment. At its heart, voodoo is an assemblage of survival lore. Science fiction would rather like to think of itself as that, too.

For the writer interested in exploring routes to what might be called transcendent survivalism, voodoo is therefore rather like catnip. *Green Eyes* is neither the first nor has it been the last science fiction novel whose author has become intoxicated with that lure; several have appeared since its first publication in the United States in 1984 as a paperback original. Chatto and Windus's hardback release of the book [in 1986] makes available in permanent form the best, if not the most orderly or most sustained, of these explorations in the pragmatics of staying alive during times of unrest. If it is more a symptom of these times than a manual for dealing with them, *Green Eyes* may all the same stand as a harbinger of survival treatises to come.

Times Literary Supplement//20 June 1986

3/William Gibson

It is impossible not to remember Alfred Bester on first gazing into William Gibson's *Neuromancer* (Ace Special, 1984). Thirty years ago the author of *The Stars My Destination* (aka *Tiger Tiger*) seemed streetwise to the future, just as Mr Gibson does right now. Both writers have their eyelids pasted open to the great forward and abysm of the new words which they world — or the other way round, if you think it's mimesis rather than sleight-of-hand.

Yanked from a Japanese slum, where he's been trying to repair his damaged nervous system and re-enter cyberspace as a cowboy and steal data from the great glowing subjective geometrics that represent corporate hotcores, Case soon finds himself way out of his depth in Turkey, in the Sprawl (a neatish term for the long predicted Boston-Atlanta megalopolis) and in Lagrange habitats out (as with Gully Foyle) in corporation-dominated interplanetary space. And if Case is out of his depth, so, soon enough, is Gibson; or, rather, the book soon escapes into genre hyperboles and schlock metaphysics, and he never tries to claw it back.

Case has been hired to penetrate the adamantine ICE (Intrusion Counter-measures Electronics) that encase the weird Lagrange-based Tessier-Ashpool corporation whose two AIs (Artificial Intelligences) turn out to be operating the whole show, for reasons of their own, which they moon about as the book closes in mooshy apotheosis. (Jupiter is not mentioned, neither of the AIs really lives in disembodied form within the psychedelic ecstasy of a gas-storm on Jupiter — but both of them, Wintermute and the eponymous Neuromancer, sound as if they *should.*) Gibson has gotten run away with by a very silly genre plot, and it's rather a shame.

Mainly because the texture of the book is so superb. Dense with the haecceity and wind of the "future." Funny, sly, engulfing. To Bester add T J Bass and Ron Cobb and the New York subway system graffiti matrix and perhaps James Tiptree Jr, and it comes clear that *Neuromancer* was conceived in a dense nutrient soup. In the mind's eye explosions: soup flying everywhere: keep Gibson from dumb quest plots that read like tv pilots for tax-loss mini-series, and he'll write one or two of the best books of the coming decade.

Interzone//Winter 1984/85

For anyone who was both impressed by his first novel and at the same time slightly embarrassed by *Neuromancer*'s garnering of all too many of the all too many awards the duckpond splashes each year onto each year's official waterproof duck, the publication of William Gibson's second novel must have been awaited with some apprehension, because too much success, whether or not an author actually touted for the chromium stars of fame, reeks of hubris, and the glistening Hugo Duck of 1985 might therefore well and deservedly bellyflop in 1986. Fortunately for those sympathetic with Gibson's plight, *Count Zero* (Gollancz, 1986), his second novel, has appeared without much delay, and does the primary thing it is most important that all second novels do: it exists. More than that, it is a good professional job of work. It is more neatly constructed than *Neuromancer*, staying more effectively within the boundaries of the game it sets itself to play; and it is inherently more modest. Mr Gibson is no Prat Icarus.

All the same, *Count Zero* is unlikely to have anything like the impact of the earlier book. It is, to begin with, set in the world of *Neuromancer* a decade or so later, and the rough novelty of that world, as first experienced, seems altogether too smoothly deft and syncromesh in its depiction second time round, so that what read as streetwise in 1985 seems all too Designer Cyberpunk a year later. It would be cruel to blame Mr Gibson for this loss of rawness, however: not only does the duck-pond market forcibly mandate tales set in a milch of pheromones (or rules of configuration) that tell the reader he/she's in the recognizeable world of sequellae [see "Trope Exposure" for an *entirely different* vocabulary describing the same phenomenon *1986*], not only does Mr Gibson therefore exude ant-pong like virtually every other writer in the genre, he also gives every appearance of believing he is telling something like the truth. The world of both *Neuromancer* and *Count Zero* — like the much simpler world of Ridley Scott's *Alien* — is an archaeology of spent momentums, but it is not only that. As a register of the cacophony that obtains in a complex world whose inhabitants, of all categories of human destiny, use the same toilet to shit in, Mr Gibson's model is apt, flexible, mantric, grave, off-hand, blank and black. It is a world whose victim/citizen/dancers inhabit a coercive grid-work of hi- and low-tech stigmata out of the nightmare of Levi-Strauss, where Sprawl and desert and L5s and AIs and the *Mu* hegemony of new/old Japan all combine into a cancer of mutual haunting, just like today doubled. It is a world of amphibolies going bang in a nightmare where the ancient is new, Gondwanaland is cyberspace. Mr Gibson can be forgiven, by those who feel he is trying to tell the truth, for trying to tell the same truth twice.

The triple spiral of the plot is more of a problem, maybe. It is surely less original in effect than the world it draws dovetailing lines through. And there is a sense of moral elusiveness, it may be, in the consummate generic through-composition of every character in the novel; Mr Gibson puts on rules of generic legibility like a coat of many colours, and the reader can end up feeling something like vertigo at the result: because every character comes across as a swift smooth automated assemblage of genre rules, we end up lacking a sense of the opinion of the book. Certainly it is the case that some folk are angry, some do the dirt on others, some have aesthetic senses, some revel in power, and so forth: but there is finally a sense that Mr Gibson is too knowing about his febrile mannikins, that, in *Count Zero,* he permits the human beast no mysteries. There is, to repeat, a great deal of telling graphic action in the book, but no drama.

The three stories are pretty complicated, and tangle themselves together dextrously. Turner, a creature ponging with the ambience of the California private-eye loner genre, is hired to supervise the obtaining of Maas Biolabs' biochip technology, ends up in the Sprawl (Boston-Atlanta) with a daughter-moll. Marly, a creature irradiated with mini-series skin-glow, finds herself hired by the immensely wealthy Josef Virek to track down the artist who has created some extraordinary object-collages. Count Zero, who longs to pong of the streets but desperately needs the wisdom he only very slowly gains, is seconded to help recover some numinous technology. As in Lucius Shepard's *Green Eyes*, a pantheon of highly pragmatic, non-theological, ultimately unmysterious voodoo entities inhabit the substrate of the world itself, which, in *Count Zero*, is, of course, cyberspace. There are twists, terrors, lots of action. If there is something lacking, it is the sense that the cast are a series of claptraps (ie tricks to gain applause of audience or of oneself), that they cannot introspect, or gain their souls.

So there may be something lacking. It may also be that Mr Gibson was not attempting to shape his text to utter certain kinds of humanistic piety. It is surely the case that humanistic assertion can come cheap, can emit just as surely as any genre claptrap the ant-pong of adherence to sets of rules for making words mean acceptable things. And underneath the pragmatic vacancy at the heart of Mr Gibson's hirelings, there is a hard stubborn insouciance; if they lack autonomy as souls, they do display, like acrobats in their cage of pheromones, a certain sprezzatura, grace under pressure. It is not perhaps surprising, given the genre's interminable triumphalism about the human animal, how little credit is given to the concept that there may be something significantly joyful in sprezzatura, and in the comprehension of fictional creatures who manage to survive, without compunction but gracefully. (How often does the merest whiff of wit or pragmatism tell Captain Kirk that a whole planet should not be allowed to perish for the sake of freedom and democracy? Never. How many SF Tricksters can sneak unaltered out of the backside of the books that entail them without becoming shamans, climbing the world-tree, returning with the grub, dying for us all but not really dying at all, becoming Dad? Not many.) Because the dancing hirelings of William Gibson's novels are not supposed to survive. In echt sf, it is the hero who survives, not the survivor.

Nothing good comes out of the fin-de-siecle decadent aesthetical pages of *Count Zero*, except the intricacy of its passage in the night. It is a cheap shocker full of old tricks and sleaze, and a thing of beauty, and a more than moderately good read. Goodness has nothing to do with it.

Foundation//May 1986

18//Robert Aickman/1914-1981

In 1955, in some obscurity, there was published in the United Kingdom a concise paperback guide to the picturesque English canal system, then as now severely threatened by the march of Progress. Robert Aickman, the author of *Know Your Waterways*, and co-founder of the Inland Waterways Association in 1946, was by the time he wrote his guide a man over forty. He had already made some kind of mark in several fields of endeavor, had already argued himself into a systematic disdain for most of the nineteenth century and all of the twentieth, and was just at the point of launching himself into what was to be his final career; for it was also in 1955 that he published "Ringing the Changes," his fifth tale of the supernatural, and began to attract widespread though bemused notice as a writer of fiction. Before his death in 1981, Aickman would publish forty more stories, a novel, and a superb autobiography; he would have become the finest English writer of supernatural fiction of the past fifty years. But from the very first he wrote as a mature man who had already experienced and, by his own testimony, suffered much.

The green cover of *Know Your Waterways* centrally frames a small photograph of a barge being steered in our direction along a tree-lined canal by a man with thick hair and glasses. Squatting or lying on this barge, and seemingly attentive to him, are two figures. It is possible they are women. But we can see only the backs of their heads. Littered about them are visible the makings of an ornate meal, an open purse, a large canister with Romany markings. In the background, at a point where the trees seem to meet over the sunshot canal, a dark shape rather like a gondola seems to be following the barge, though there is no sign that the helmsman has any full awareness of this shadowing. He is instead responding to the intrusion of the camera; his mien is assured, seemingly competent, but in the strong glare of the sun it is an oddly exposed countenance, as though something were about to crumble. It is of course impossible to say what. Although he is not identified in any way, it is clear that the helmsman in the photograph is Aickman himself.

Two women together whose relationship with one another may not be clear; a helmsman of their company, but at the same time isolated, perhaps by age; a stretch of seemingly navigable water encroached upon by undergrowth; Romany runes; a mysterious doppelganger shape as deep into the background as it is possible to discern; exposing sunlight and intrusive shadow, Mammon and Styx: the effect may be accidental, but in this photograph, which features a man whom we recognize from later dustjackets but who is not here named, we are thrust directly into the complexly ominous universe of Aickman's fiction. Just as in that fiction Aickman's own life everywhere shows through, so in this photograph one can sense a welling up of personal significance from everything hinted at or half-stifled or merely visible, for in the urgent pregnancy of Aickman's tales everything signifies, everything contributes to the quest for the terrible secret meaning of the world.

Aickman published his very first supernatural fiction as late as 1951, so that the composition of almost all of his tales would in all likelihood seem to postdate what Carl Gustav Jung identified as the midlife crisis, that complex of troubles which, in his view, afflicts for a time any normal adult who has lived long enough to pass through the glorious dawn when a guise of youthful heroism was the appropriate response to challenge. Understandably, most writers of popular fiction concentrate on this first period, and are generally reluctant to extend their interest into the time of staleness or hidden retribution (as in the tragedy of Oedipus) that succeeds — that shadows — the moments of triumph. But in the real world, after he has returned home with his tribute and his gift of knowledge and his long scars, the hero must then be prepared to face the crisis of his midlife, or die in nescience. For a time his heroic past will seem full of sound and fury, his present life will seem intolerably arid and void of novelty, and the future will lack any conceivable meaning. At this stage the hero may divorce his wife, lay waste a much younger woman, plunge into a new career.

For Jung, though we are certainly putting words into his mouth, the hero's psyche has now become a kind of battlefield, a Waste Land through which the archetypes that figured and inspired the exploits of his youth jostle sourly for advantage. If he is to pass through his crisis, the ageing hero must somehow integrate these discordant aspects of his personality into the full harmonious "individuation" of the mature Jungian self; he must somehow transform these clamorous images of internecine warfare into a kind of *chivalry*, like Arthur he must create a Round Table for the knights of his domain. Only thus integrated can he face the most important remaining challenge which awaits in the dusk of the flesh — which is death — with equanimity.

But if a man fails to become something like King Arthur to himself, then he will be haunted, for when the archetypes appropriate to young manhood fail to integrate into a mature selfhood, they then tend to manifest themselves in the form of ghosts. It is primarily in this sense — a reading in which the world itself becomes the deranged battlefield of the self — that so many of Aickman's finest efforts can be read as ghost stories. If it is at the heart of fantasy to treat the objective world as a manifestation or diorama of the subjective, then it is a matter of niggling interpretation to judge whether the ghosts in an Aickman story are objective or subjective in nature. And if the typical Aickman ghosting represents a failure on its victim's part to construct out of the jarring cohorts of his psyche a selfhood that makes any sense, then it can come as no surprise to find that many of his stories are virtually indecipherable, that by their very nature they resist paraphrase. In an Aickman story it is sufficient that the victim recognize the nightmare world he inhabits, which inhabits him; by definition, *understanding* the world is beyond him. For if he understood he would be Arthur.

Many come to their midlife crises; few come through them. Whether Aickman himself gained in these terms the repose of full adulthood it would be impertinent to question, though he very clearly hints throughout *The Attempted Rescue* (1966), his significantly titled autobiography to the age of 25 or so, that he did not judge himself to have gained anything like equipoise in later life. What is surely clear is that his fiction is conceived from the other side of heroism, and that he is almost unique in this. His stories come to us from a distant shore, though it is one we must attempt to descry; nor is the life of the teller of those tales at all easy to pin down.

Despite occasional episodes of self-exposure, of which the autobiography is the most prominent, Robert Fordyce Aickman remains a figure of some obscurity to the literary world. It seems deliberate. Although *The Attempted Rescue*, for example, clearly ties his childhood in to the period dominated by World War One, and supplies sufficient internal evidence for one to establish his year of birth as 1914, nowhere in the book is that date given, nor did it appear in biographical summaries while Aickman was alive. Facts do emerge, all the same. He was born in London, England. He was an only child. His parents were affluent, though not excessively so. His maternal grandfather was the popular novelist Richard Marsh, now best known as the author of *The Beetle* (1897). Other relatives were even more eminent Victorians than this, and Aickman spent long periods visiting large imposing residences, the like of which haunt his fiction from beginning to end. He attended several private schools with outward success, though he was deeply unhappy. (This is of course an obsessive leit-motif of English autobiography.) He discovered the theatre, and developed a life-long obsession with opera. He began to write, publishing "a toy pagoda of words" called "What is a Flounce?" in the *New English Weekly* in 1934. But then he gave up writing. He had a variety of jobs. He became theatre critic of *The Nineteenth Century and After.* His childhood obsession with travel blossomed into the founding of the Inland Waterways Association, which lobbied for the preservation of England's webbing of narrow dank "useless" canals. He was either founder or a moving force in several other associations, including the London Opera Society. At some point he married and divorced. He was heterosexual. His relationships with women were numerous and intense; with men he got along less well. With Elizabeth Jane Howard — each writing three stories independently — he published a first collection, *We Are for the Dark*, in 1951, obscurely. In 1964 he edited with great success *The Fontana Book of Great Ghost Stories*, producing seven sequels by 1972. Before his death eight further volumes of fiction appeared; a posthumous volume appeared in 1985. He died in 1981, at the age of 66.

It all seems to have meant little or nothing, as *The Attempted Rescue* makes clear:

> For years I seem to have regarded myself as what F R Rolfe called a Nowt: a being without independent volition, directed wholly by circumstances and the will of others. If the circumstances were right (which was very infrequently), I could shine in a moment, and rise too, but I could do nothing to penetrate or to discover these circumstances. I was as the clown in a French mime; with wild hair in place

> of long sleeves. I turned almost all my suffering inwards, until it became unbearable, because nothing ever happened, neither break-out nor breakdown, so that I never ceased to bear it. Doubtless the suffering was unconsciously purposive, in the true neurotic fashion. The only possibility in my mind was that I might become an author.

As his autobiography also makes clear, Aickman was convinced that much of his suffering lay in his failure to escape the living and posthumous influence of his extraordinary parents. He was intensely devoted to his supple, delicate, frustrated mother, and lived in terror of his monstrously domineering, eccentric, clockwork father; indeed, by quoting Samuel Butler in the "Proem" to his autobiography, Aickman makes it clear that he conceived of his life as bearing anxious witness to the parent/son catastrophe depicted in *The Way of All Flesh* (1903). His father, who appears in various guises throughout the fiction, was by nature mechanical and impulsive, time-bound and insanely dilatory, a figure locked into lunatic clashes of obsession like a robot bound to simultaneous conflicting programmes. Supremely deficient in human integration (or chivalry), Aickman's father, like a deranged archetype, clearly haunted his life and suffuses his work. Unmistakeable portraits of him occur in "The Inner Room" (1966) and in "The Fetch" (1980), the first of the two late novelettes which comprise in coded form an autobiographical summa; in its proper place we will speak of "The Stains" (1980), the second of these stores, in which ghosts are laid and death embraced.

In "The Fetch" no such reconciliation is possible. "In all that matters, I was an only child, " the narrator of the tale begins, and draws a portrait of a personality irretrievably locked into bondage to his own childhood and to the family "fetch," whom (though he denies "her") he cannot escape. His father seems to be "a wraith with a will and power that no one available could resist." His mot her is deeply adoring but dies while he is a child, under horrific circumstances, after a visitation from the fetch, the doppelganger-like witch who comes to one who must die and who shows him, in its hooded visage, his own face. From this point his father abandons him utterly (but owns him still). Like a vulnerable helmsman beginning his transit of something ominously like the Styx, the narrator spends the remainder of his life affirming and denying the terms that define him. "I had long recognized that many people would have said that I was obsessed. But the whole business emed to me the explanation of my being." He goes through the motions of a career. He falls desperately in love and marries, but the fetch comes for his wife. His second wife, refusing any credence to that which binds him, isolates him all the more. His life is a shambles and an imprisonment. Finally he retreats to the deserted family seat in rural Scotland, and the fetch comes for him at last. But he barricades the doors and windows of his domain, so as not to see his own face. When the story ends, he is still alive, which is heroism of a sort. It is misplaced, however. Youthful heroism will not solve the crisis of a soul in extremis, for the narrator has failed to live; and his survival is an ironic jape, for neither can he face his death.

Aickman is quite explicit about his sense of the nature of supernatural manifestations. Introducing *The Fontana Book of Great Ghost Stories* (1964), he makes clear his lack of interest in random sensation:

> The ghosts are the returned dead whom once we knew, or our uncle knew. They are creatures we once knew, but now know no more .... They are, occasionally, creatures we never knew (or think we didn't), like angels or devils or toys possessed by a spirit. They are things within us which we have, as psychologists say, projected outside us. They are little children beating on the glass. They are free; at least from us. They are real. *We are glad to meet them when we are glad to meet ourselves, but that is to be one man (or woman) marked out of ten thousand.* [My italics]

There is much that is inexplicable in his nearly 50 stories, but very little that is truly arbitrary, because the terrible secret meaning of the ghost-ridden world of Aickman's fiction lies precisely in its binding complicity, for by the sign that you fail to understand it (having failed to be glad to meet yourself) the world *means* what you have become. It is therefore a fiction of consequences. If you have failed to become chivalrous to the knowledge of the approach of death, then you will end up as much a ghost as that which haunts you. If (as then must be the case) you fail to understand the world that mirrors — that means — the Waste Land of your fragmented psyche, the world will not for that reason cease to bind you. Truly it will be otherwise.

Sometimes clearly, sometimes permutated into bizarre cacophonies of symbol and event that seem to mock paraphrase, this sustaining moral import can be perceived throughout Aickman's work. At times, as in "The Insufficient Answer" (1951), or "Choice of Weapons" (1964), or "Ravissante" (1968), the internecine warfare between self and world may be too jangled for the reader easily to parse. The insistent striving for meaningfulness of his fiction is perhaps more poignantly effective in what might be called the tales of failed transcendance, those stories whose protagonists are compelled by their sense of inward crisis to attempt to change their lives, perhaps utterly. They set out on doomed journeys, as in "The Inner Room," already mentioned, which is a virtual maze of journeys into the mirror, with no exit. They come to islands, as in "The View" (1951) or "Just a Song at Twilight" (1965) or "The Wine-Dark Sea" (1966), only to find their sense of exile supernaturally confirmed. In "No Time is Passing" (1980), a river suddenly discovered at the foot of the protagonist's garden demands of him that he cross it; but the god or monstrous parody of a man who rules the other side sends him scurrying back across the exact same river, for nothing has changed, and he remains caught in the petty, unchivalrous, cushioned shambles of his life. In "The Hospice" (1976), which offers a horrific and hilarious vision of the aesthetic and human costs of living in the heat-death of modern middle-class de-industrialized England, a traveler is lured into confronting a death probably identical to his own, for which "he should not have to wait long. " The grounds of the sanitorium for insomniacs in "Into the Wood" (1968) draws the sleepless protagonist into a forest advertised as transcendent; but it is no more than a labyrinth which returns one to the institution. A similar confirmation of impoverishment awaits the woman in "The Next Glade" (1980), who is drawn into the woods by a phantom lover but finds only her failed marriage there.

The significance of these terminal landscapes is not exhausted, moreover, by their manifestation of the only vistas possible to those stymied by crisis; for the typical Aickman protagonist inhabits a Waste Land whose origin and contours additionally represent a complex vision of the failure of Western civilization to sustain, through its artifacts and its imperial progress, an organic human dimension. It is worth noting that, at about the time Aickman was beginning to write fiction, the cultural climate of postWar England had begun to facilitate critical recovery of the social thought of one of the gravest of nineteenth century prophets of the cancerous elephantiasis of our decline, John Ruskin (1819-1900). As Sir Kenneth Clark, speaking of Ruskin's magisterial abhorrence of industrial "values, " put it in *The Listener* for 1 April 1948:

> We do not yet believe in the greatest of all his truths: than any ugly lamp-post is a wicked lamp-post. We are all inclined to take ugliness for granted, as something which has always existed and for which we are not responsible .... [But], every form we create will betray us; and to the sensitive eye our utility furnishings will tell their tales as surely as if they were covered with flowers and scrolls or embossed views of the Forth Bridge.

In *The Attempted Rescue*, Aickman puts it this way: "Possibly, as Wilde suggested, the awful truth is that appearances are true."

A conviction that appearances are indeed terrifyingly true is manifest throughout the fiction, clearly underpinning the sense (previously argued) that the world, for an Aickman character, means what it says. Limned in a prose whose elaborate mandarin irony barely masks exorbitant disgust, this marriage of appearance and truth effectively puts into the terms of fiction the nub of Ruskin's thought; and so far as they are to be deciphered from his ceaseless vigilance about self-revelation, Aickman's political inclinations also seem to reflect Ruskin's: "I am . . ." Ruskin says in *Praeterita* (1886), "a violent Tory of the old school; — Walter Scott's school, that is to say, and Homer's."

From *We Are For the Dark* (1951) down to the last tales, we find ourselves always in the hall of mirrors of a world shaped by these convictions, recounted in the same fixated tone of voice. It is not a simple nor a young man's world. The voice is the voice of a Roman at the end of Empire, Claudianus's perhaps (d408). It is the voice of a man finally unable to direct his consuming rage at our loss of virtue into works of a scope ample enough to express it. Stories which are clear allegories of our current cultural straits — like "Growing Boys" and "Residents Only" (both 1977) — tend to disintegrate into sour skits, and the unremitting irony of their telling comes close to sanctimony and carping. In the extraordinary complexity of the intellectual and emotional repertory he brings to bear on his fiction, Aickman may evoke comparison with a writer such as Thomas Mann, rather than with any predecessor in the field of supernatural fiction proper. But any such comparison does expose the limits of his imaginative hold. In Mann's only major novel of supernatural import, *Doctor Faustus* (1947), a repertory not dissimilar to Aickman's undergoes a scouring ironical metamorphosis into an aesthetic shape so encompassing that we can descry within it — without cramping or piety or shortcuts into sarcasm — a full vision of the fate of Western man. Aickman's mind may well be as complex as Mann's, but its concinnity is short of breath (unlike Mann's encompassing shapeliness), and its lack of a grasp sufficient to its reach can be seen in the failure of *The Late Breakfasters* (1964), his only novel to be published while he was alive. Its supernatural content (a lissome ghost) is flimsy and soon dissipates; in its coquettish figurations of stylish writing it registers as apprentice work (the date of composition is unknown); and it breaks down into two mismatched halves, with an effect almost of mincing: Firbank and water. After this, Aickman never published a story longer than 25,000 words.

Of these stories, there are several highly polished professional tales that stand rather to one side. That they are his most popular work may demonstrate Aickman's intelligence as a craftsman. "The Waiting Room" (1956) adroitly traps a lost traveler in a waiting room built over a burial ground for hanged felons; he awakens with a bad crick in his neck. "Ringing the Changes" (1955), the most reprinted but far from the best of all Aickman's stories, introduces a newly married couple to an isolated village in the East Anglian fens on the night the dead are awakened by the sound of all the church bells ringing at once; the ensuing imbroglio obscurely sours the new marriage. "Pages from a Young Girl's Journal" (1973), which won a World Fantasy Award, details the young girl's unfolding awareness that she has been changed into a vampire by a dark stranger she met at the ball. Set in Italy, and featuring cameo roles for both Byron and Shelley, it is a vivid period masquerade. Aickman's impersonation of the young English girl is deftly marmoreal, chillingly virtuoso. These tales may strike a traditional note for the reader of supernatural fiction; given Aickman's complex seriousness of intention as a writer, and what seems in his latter years the financial freedom to write as he wished, it is not surprising that few of those stories yet unmentioned much resemble them. The bulk of his canon (as we've said) speaks from the other shore: from the end of Empire and its heroisms.

It is with *Dark Entries* (1964) that Aickman makes his first wide impact as an independent author (the stories in the volume with Elizabeth Jane Howard were, confusingly, not individually ascribed to either writer, with a blurring effect on both). Beyond "Ringing the Changes," "The Waiting Room" and "The View," it contains, in "Bind Your Hair" (1964), a fantasia on the theme of the *rite de passage* that is both funny and alarming. In sequences reminiscent of Ivy Compton Burnett, we see that the engagement of Clarinda to Dudley is faltering because of his fatal lack of sexual affect, so that it is impossible for her to envisage any meaningful passage into a different order of human existence. The supernatural intervenes, in the form of a bacchanalian fertility rite in a sacred grove which casts together old gods, middle-aged gypsies, young children, and the stalled tremulous Clarinda. At the story's end, still with the blank Dudley, she remains poised at the brink of a genuine passage, though we are left free to doubt — as with so many Aickman characters — that she will ever make a move to save her life.

Along with the political satire and soul-bondage of "My Poor Friend," the numbing social backdrop of "A Roman Question" and the metaphysical slapstick of "Larger Than Oneself," *Powers of*

Darkness (1966) also contains, in "The Visiting Star" (all stories are 1966), Aickman's most complex transformation of his vast knowledge of the theatre. In a barren Midlands city, as cold Christmas approaches, an assortment of provincial types awaits the arrival of Arabella Rokeby, a great star from a time impossibly remote. Preceded by her agent, whose name (Superbus) reflects his tyrannical nature, she soon enchants everyone, as though she were something magical, as though she literally incarnated the thaumaturgy of true theatre. And indeed this is the case. Any actor wears masks; but Rokeby is nothing more (or less) than an intricately wedded procession of masks, a mannikin of Superbus, a psychic vampire. All the same, and very movingly, she remains humble in face of the art she serves so completely. After hints of ritual extravagances and depths, and after a catastrophe that ushers in Christmas, the magical breathtaking show (which she has come to star in) does go on.

As we have noted, many Aickman stories present the failure to achieve an integrated world in terms of attempted transcendental journeys, as though into a better future. In a second broad category, usually signaled by someone's arrival at a meticulously described house, the attempted rescue has already failed by the time the tale begins, and within the house will be discovered an inverse ghost, a mummy, perhaps still breathing. One of the better examples of this category is "The House of the Russians, " in which the central house is on an island: doubly mazed. Also first published in *Sub Rosa* (1968) is "The Unsettled Dust, " probably the finest of these stories of frozen belatedness. Its narrator, who represents a controlling bureaucracy, visits one of the stately homes under his aegis, where he finds everything covered with dust, and the two resident sisters (they're the home's former owners) locked into an icy covert feud whose source he inadvertantly uncovers when he too finds himself being haunted by the ghost of the young man one of them had long ago attempted to elope with. His mysterious death has frozen all life in their persons. There is no passage for them, no resolution of their sibling warfare, no future. As the ghost runs through its fixed reiteration of the tragedy, dust is briefly unsettled; but when the ghost has passed, there is once again dead silence:

> And, interestingly enough, the dust had by then ceased to swirl, though I am sure it still lay thick on the room floor, the floors of all the other rooms, the passages, the stairs, the furniture, and all our hearts.

"Meeting Mr Millar" (1972), "The Same Dog" (1974) and "The Clock Watcher" (1974), all from *Cold Hand in Mine* (1976), and "Compulsory Games" (1976), "Wood" (1976) and "*Le Miroir*," all from *Tales of Love and Death* (1977) are also stories of psychic mummification. As we near the end of Aickman's career, we find that his figures of horrific immobility, whatever their ostensible age or sex, become more profoundly estranged from human kind, more desperately caught into that clockwork of obsessive reiteration which disqualifies them from genuine being and from genuine death (it is remarkable how few of Aickman's trapped protagonists ever actually manage to die); more and more they come to resemble his dreadful father. In both "Meeting Mr Millar" and "Wood," characters who at first seem no more than psychic mummies (but still human) are revealed (horrifyingly) as *literal* clockwork, simulacra savagely mocking of human nature in their fixed reiteration of human traumas, human longings for change, growth, redemption; nor can they die. The most impressive of these stories is probably the superb "Compulsory Games," in which failed transcendance and mummification conjoin in deadly wedlock. Colin has lived too mildly, too cautiously, ignoring the world as it changes; though in this story not literally so, Colin is a mummy, and ignorant of his condition. His wife suddenly leaves him for someone real, and the charade of his trivial existence collapses into a succession of unendurable ghostings. The world becomes a deranged and gloating nightmare, in which he must recognize his own shattered being, but from which he cannot escape. "He was being mashed up and transmogrified before his own inner eyes; and the new entity, deprived of all egoism, would live for ever." For Colin, there is no passage. For us, his fate has a wider significance in that the Waste Land to which "the new smiling Colin" is abandoned wears the hectic lineaments of the Modern World.

It is apparently the case that Aickman was unwell for several years before his death from cancer in February 1981. Though the stories in *Intrusions* (1980) are as fine as anything he wrote earlier, they speak to us in measures more deeply elegiac than before. We have already mentioned "The Fetch," "No Time is Passing" and "The Next Glade." Married in tone to these stories, though it was collected only in *Night Voices*, the posthumous (1985) grab-bag, "The Stains" (1980) can stand for all of them. Cancer is not mentioned as such, but in the inexorable suffusion of staining through this tale, stainings of body and world, we recognize an irreversible and growing consanguinity with death. At the same time, "The Stains" is also a story of redemptive love, a *Liebestod*. Stephen's wife has died of an unspecified disease, and he visits his feckless brother in the bleak North of England, ostensibly to recuperate. Walking alone on the moors, he sees an oread or mountain-nymph at the end of the visible path. Her name is Nell (knell). He is stricken with love for her, though a great stain on her body affrights him. To wrap up his affairs they go to London, which seems fungoid. The world is indeed disintegrating. But they escape for the moment, making their way back to a secret dwelling in the heart of the moor, where Nell's dread father — who is like death, and the past, but also like the natural world beyond our psychoses — begins to shake the earth in his search for them. He will not be gainsaid. The stain on Nell's body has migrated to Stephen's, where it belongs. But he has been happy with her, and for a time he has "counted the good things only, as does a sundial." At the heart of their secret home is a stone slab, and under it a small room, "more a coffer than a room, Stephen apprehended." Here, as the father breathes stertorously outside, they come indissolubly together, married. Stephen is, of course, dead.

Most remarkable in this tale is the sense it imparts of an earned reconciliation between Stephen and a world engorged with stains; redemptively, he has been capable of greeting its terminal message in the shape of Nell. She is the very image of chivalry. It is Aickman's sole successful marriage; and quite possibly his only genuine death. If he wrote further stories, they have not been published. It is not, in any case, easy to comprehend that a man may reach much closer to the other side of the Styx, and tell the tale.

We Are For the Dark: Six Ghost Stories. London: Jonathan Cape, 1951. With Elizabeth Jane Howard.

The Late Breakfasters. London: Victor Gollancz, 1954.

Dark Entries. London: Collins, 1964.

Powers of Darkness. London: Collins, 1964.

Sub Rosa: Strange Tales. London: Gollancz, 1968.

Cold Hand in Mine: Eight Strange Stories. London: Gollancz, 1975 (for 1976).

Tales of Love and Death. London: Gollancz, 1977.

Painted Devils. New York: Scribners, 1979. A compilation from previous volumes.

Intrusions: Strange Tales. London: Gollancz, 1980.

Night Voices: Strange Stories. London: Gollancz, 1985.

E.F. Bleiler, ed. *Supernatural Fiction Writers; Fantasy and Horror.* (Scribners, 1985)

[Ev Bleiler is a wise and considerate editor, and for the 18 or so pieces I wrote for him in the 1980s for two of his books he made only the most tactful — and unanswerable — suggestions for changes. In the essay here printed on Robert Aickman, for instance, he thought I had spent about two pages too long on Jungian archetypes, and suggested that I had begun to repeat myself. He was perfectly right, I cut the superfluous passages, and they do not appear here. If this essay does differ in some particulars from the version Scribners published, it is because (against Ev's continued objections) that firm used house (and hired-in) copy editors to "clean up" manuscripts *after* Ev had approved them. Though contributors were given copies of their edited manuscripts, and allowed to reinstate their original wordings, it was of course impractical (and would, I suppose, have been impolitic) to have tried to restore every single wording to its original state. I have of course gone back to my original typescript for the version now printed — though some small improvements have been made to that original. Scribners, by the way, was bought by Macmillans just before *Supernatural Fiction Writers* was due to appear, and it's pretty obvious that Macmillans did not have their heart in the book. It was released invisibly; review copies were like hens' teeth; dealers were refused discounts; and the book has hardly been seen by anyone, which is a great shame. Ev Bleiler worked extremely hard on the project, as did the many writers like myself, who helped supply the 150 essays making up its ample two volumes *1986.*]

17//Gene Wolfe:

1982.

After years of solid productive work, Gene Wolfe has suddenly become a very prominent writer indeed (it's about time) and very marketable (but he's a grown man and won't OD). All the same, even at this celebratory moment, it's hard not to cavil at the title of his latest collection, *Gene Wolfe's Book of Days* (Doubleday, 1981), and the procrustean hype inevitably generated by the notion it presents that eighteen previously autonomous stories can usefully be brought together to illustrate a chronology of Days like Valentine's Day and Mother's Day and Thanksgiving and so on. Appended to work of the complexity Wolfe here deposes, these labels, like stool pigeons, tell versions of their tales only a cop would believe, though maybe a kind of sly irony is being offered here, because if there's one thing Wolfe's work is not, it's simpleminded.

Certainly some of the stories in this volume seem a bit garish and one-dimensional when associated with deeply worked achievements like "Forlesen" and "Three Million Square Miles." "How I Lost the Second World War . . . , " for instance, or "Of Relays and Roses," are both pretty much what they seem to be: gimcrack genre notions stretched out to cope with some magazine or other's routine space requirements. When he's being as straightforward as he's capable of, Wolfe is no more than competent, and indeed his virtues tend to turn a little sour. Indirection can become misdirection; richness of language and thematic multivalency can so overload simple narrative resolutions that the reader ends the story with the thought that maybe a final page is missing, because his eyes have been opened too wide.

Fortunately, Wolfe very rarely tries his hand with what one might call the stoolpigeon story — the kind of story you can paraphrase and catch the truth of. When he bears down, because of his superb control over and enrichment of the organon of generic material (an organon one might well have thought already done to death), he reminds me just a little (I'm afraid this is going to sound pretty pretentious) of Johann Sebastian Bach. The central fact about Bach is *not* his originality (for in Romantic terms he was not very original) but his immense comprehensive grasp of the given. As Bach synthesized the Baroque just as it entered heat-death, so Gene Wolfe seems to be attempting to synthesize true stories out of the growing incoherence of our own genre.

It is not the notes of a fugue but their echoes that give meaning. Clearly inclined to irony and parody, both being techniques which of course require an already existing Matter to work upon and to draw echoes out of, Gene Wolfe has for years been quietly but implacably re-naturing the shibboleth- and gizmo-ridden deep structures of our genre, bringing out the internal human circumstances that have always monitored our flights to Mars, however tenuously they were dealt with by overworked "hack" writers trying to feed themselves at a cent a word. At the heart of his best stories (it is the actual subject matter of the astonishing "Forlesen") lies a remarkable ability to create adequate breathing-models of the experience of moving from childhood to adulthood, from adulthood to old age. In these stories a deeply attuned vision of the rhythms and outcomes of the life-conversation between child and family, between adult and world, gives meaning to both "sides," tells us ultimately that maybe there are no real "sides" in the conversations we all have with the voices of those near to us and with the prison of the world whose depiction in science fiction terms is at the same time hilarious and minatory in Wolfe's hands; no sides perhaps, but certainly walls.

As a writer Wolfe is avid for meaning; he clearly longs to make the world *mean* something human. But unlike too many contemporary writers in the field — for whom the search for meaning is for a door in the wall through which readers can be piped for a price into the secret garden — Wolfe tells us again and again that understanding is going to have to be its own reward. That there is no other prize. That there is no one to give us a prize for knowing that we have been alive. After a lifetime which has passed with the passing of a single day, Forlesen has a question to ask of the undertaker who has magically appeared:

> "I want to know if it's meant anything," Forlesen said. "If what I suffered — if it's been worth it."
> "No," the little man said. "Yes. No. Yes. Yes. No. Yes. Yes. Maybe."

The Magazine of Fantasy and Science Fiction//February 1982

1983.

It is not a title to win converts. But now that we have *The Citadel of the Autarch* (Timescape/Simon and Schuster, 1983), fourth and final volume of Gene Wolfe's superb long science fiction novel, *The Book of the New Sun*, perhaps we can be allowed to forget *The Shadow of the Torturer* and *The Claw of the Conciliator* and *The Sword of the Lictor* (all separately reviewed in *Book World* over the past three years), and to forget this current title, which is confusingly interchangeable with those that misrepresent its three predecessors, and from now on think of the novel as a whole, under the continuing subtitle which defines it as such. For *The Book of the New Sun*, all 400,000 grave and polished words of it, is far greater than the sum of its parts. [This was written before Gene Wolfe argued the case for his individual titles on grounds that seem perfectly reasonable, but which do not answer the case, roughly hinted at above, that those individual titles are significantly wrong in tone, implying as they do yet another high-fantasy hyper-ventilation show, and opening the door for critical bloopers like David Wingrove's, who contributes to *Trillion Year Spree*, main author Brian W Aldiss, the following critical exercise in mouthing the foot: "Realism was never Wolfe's purpose, it must be said, but *The Book of the New Sun* owes much of its popularity to the sense one has that it is intelligent, meaningful sword and sorcery," When Wolfe reminds one that the title of the first novel refers to the fact that the Torturer stands between the

Sun and his victim, he is not managing to speak to the David Wingroves of the world, with dire consequences. *1986*] So let us call it *The Book* for short, and spend some time in praise of the new Dante.

Well not quite, perhaps. *The Book* isn't quite *The Divine Comedy* in four bumper parts instead of only three. It doesn't quite have the stature, one knows that of course, though Wolfe does have something of Dante's appalling assurance; nor does *The Book* quite manage to present a vision of reality through which an entire culture can apprehend something of the intricate passages and turnings of the Word of God as He writes It out, layer after layer. But if Gene Wolfe is to be taken seriously — and however thrilling or pleasing *The Book* may be, there is simply no point at all in thinking of its author as creator merely of a speculative entertainment — then he must be taken as attempting something analogous to Dante's supreme effort. With great urgency, layer after layer, he has created a world radiantly intrinsicate with meaning, a novel that makes sense in the end only if it is read as an attempt to represent the Word of God. How intimate — how dizzyingly remote — how comforting or alienating that Word can be, each reader will of course discover.

We are on Urth, millenia upon millenia hence. So densely impacted with millions of years of human life is this world that even commercial mines, dug however deep into the ransacked planet, produce only bone and brick and artifact and icon, layer upon layer of human meaning, most of it indecipherable at first or second glance (just like certain passages of *The Book*). So the very earth radiates significance, as do its inhabitants, who live awash in ancientness, but who seem to glow with the fabulousness of their environment, strangely youthful, strangely assured. They have the deep polish of the citizens of the legends of childhood. But Urth is dying. The sun is red; stars are visible in the dark sky of midday. The starships of earlier epochs have become the dwelling places and headquarters of guilds themselves ancient. The mountains of Urth have been carved into giant sculptures of Autarchs, themselves fossils unearthed from deep mines.

Through this labyrinth of a library of a world — for three volumes — we have followed the adventures of young Severian, journeyman Torturer in exile for allowing a "client" to kill herself too soon. It may be the case that for some readers Severian's earlier experiences may have seemed picaresque in nature, just slightly ad hoc, though colorful enough. But inexorably it becomes more and more clear that nothing in Severian's narrative — he tells the whole tale himself some time after he has become

Autarch of the land of his birth — is accidental. Everything in his life becomes substance, and the reader can feel at times a kind of sweet cold terror as the true shape of that life begins to come clear. Much that happens to Severian [from the precise point of his baptismal immersion in the waters of the Gyoll and subsequent rebirth in the first paragraph of the first volume *1986*] has been lived before (in a manner which the fourth volume reveals) and is therefore twice-told and talmudic, a code reverently to be broken. But much has *not* happened before, and represents something new on Urth. New on Urth is the Severian who will redeem humanity by becoming the New Sun/Apollo, or the New Son/Christ.

A miracle is required. The miracle (as T H White, quoting Malory, once said of Lancelot) is that Severian is allowed to perform a miracle. Early in Volume One, he has — it seems inadvertently — acquired from a passel of traveling nuns their most treasured relic, the Claw of the Conciliator. The Conciliator is a Redeemer of a past age who may come again. At first the Claw seems to be a kind of weapon, but slowly we come to realize that — in direct contradiction of all the habits of high fantasy — it does nothing but heal. And the land blossoms where Severian sleeps. Only in the fourth volume do we see that the Claw is not the miracle, that it merely releases in Severian the knowledge of his true nature. (The reader may at this point remember an episode from Volume One, long before Severian obtains the Claw. In a rubbish heap, he finds *and brings to life* a three-legged dog named Triskele — we do not know where this name comes from, for Severian does not tell us, though a little research will show that in Classical times the word triskele designated a three-legged icon used in the worship of the god Apollo — who soon disappears into the Corridors of Time within the Citadel, leaving tracks which represent the only possible route for Severian to follow, after he has become Autarch, in his search for . . . : but this is to tell the story.) He returns the Claw to its keepers. He becomes Autarch, in a scene terrible with desire and hints of the burdens to come. Animate projections from his childhood tell him something of what he must face — and it is one of the hoariest of all science fiction clichés that he will soon be pitting his wits against, but Wolfe somehow manages to transform it (as he transforms so much else) into something moving, and rich, and strange. And Severian goes to the Ocean, and stands upon the beach, where he realizes that:

> The thorn was a sacred Claw because all thorns were sacred Claws; the sand in my boots was sacred sand because it came from a beach

> of sacred sand. The cenobites treasured up the relics of the sannyasins because the sannyasins had approached the Pancreator. But everything had approached and even touched the Pancreator, because everything had dropped from his hand. Everything was a relic. All the world was a relic. I drew off my boots, that had traveled with me so far, and threw them into the waves that I might not walk shod on holy ground.

He then ascends the Throne.

Like Funes the Memorious in Borges' story, Severian cannot forget anything, though it is by no means certain that he cannot lie, so that *The Book* which tells his life is like a Theatre of Memory, where everything stands for something else, where everything is a relic. Severian's life is a performance — a rehearsing of parousia — which he cannot help but memorize for any future occasion. He needs no prompting; he writes *The Book of the New Sun* [and this may be the key to much of its disingenuousness about explosive material like the question of Severian's parentage *1986*] to prompt *us*.

Volume Four of this talmud is harrowing, but is full of pleasures as well. There are four new-minted fables set into the text, each one irradiated with the Ocean of Story. There is Master Ash, who roots Yggdrasil-like back through time to observe Severian's Urth. There is time travel, space travel, teleportation; laser duels and gentle Mammoths; delirium and dreams and the tying-up of loose threads. *The Book* is a feast and a eucharist; layer after layer, we have just begun to know it. You must read it.

The Washington Post Book World//January 1983

1983.

So. Out of the silence exile and cunning we have had delivered unto us *The Book of the New Sun*, a text which embroils its readers in a fever of interpretation and which seems designed to unpeel its layers of possible meaning more or less indefinitely until the reader begins to feel that his exegetical dance is somehow isomorphic with the true *Book* itself; and here we have something else, *The Castle of the Otter* (Ziesing Brothers, 1982 for 1983), which is subtitled with some small accuracy *A Book About the Book of the New Sun*, but which in facts deals only with the first volumes of the tetralogy, and which *seems* to be an attempt on Gene Wolfe's part to cast some light on the darker tesserae of the labyrinth he has created with such mastery.

It is not.

The Castle of the Otter is a perfectly commendable set of footnotes to the writing of a complex novel. There are touches of autobiography. There is some boasting — for once, in this duckpond, justified. Some of the symbolic connections linking the rose and the sun and the individual titles of the tetralogy are illuminated, though assuredly they are not explained. There is a glossary which unravels Wolfe's extraordinarily savvy use of obscure but existing English words to help establish that dizzying sense of distance and intimacy, antiquity and ravenous presence, by virtue of which *The Book of the New Sun*, like deja vu, seems as indecipherable as one's inmost self, that which becomes, as it is more examined, more alien. The various epigraphs and poems in the text are referred to and justified, though assuredly they are not explained. And various proper names receive the same treatment. And in a long chapter called "Cavalry in the Age of the Autarch," Mr Wolfe rides a fine hobbyhorse into the long debate on the usefulness of mounted soldiers in warfare. And there is a self-interview. And, in one chapter, in a tone hauntingly reminiscent of *The Book* itself, several of the characters of the novel tell one painful joke each.

It is all valuable enough, though too frequently Mr Wolfe sounds almost fannish in his dancelike presentation of the appearance of blameless bonhomie, but in truth *Otter* impinges not a whit upon the dense cruel serenity of Severian's twice-told disingenuous dark tale, which I (for one) am more and more coming to think of as a highly charged political apologia for his dubious (and maybe even blasphemous) assumption of the autarchy, and only secondarily a "confession" — but this is not the place for that kind of speculation. It is not Mr Wolfe's responsibility to volunteer apodictic textual confirmations (or refutations) of that kind of interpretive thought. Mr Wolfe may at some point wish to divulge (at almost random instance) his reasons for making the House Absolute isomorphic with the house of the re-cloned narrator of *The Fifth Head of Cerberus*, or he may not. More likely, he will mention that he constructed this isomorphism *in such and such a manner* — and leave the reasoning to us. Which is just. Surely it is just. It is nothing but just. But it is in the nature of any reader to long for gospel, and *The Castle of the Otter* is nothing but gloss.

So. We are not brought safe to the other side. *The Book* and the reading of *The Book* remain (that word again) isomorphic. If this makes us feel a continuing vertigo, then so be it. Vertigo occurs when the eye is stripped bare of its bachelors.

Foundation 28//July 1983

1985.

[Early in 1985, out of the blue, a certain ____________________ from New York communicated with me on a matter of real urgency, guy, to wit that the Committee for the 1985 Worldcon, to be held in Australia and called Aussiecon Two, would be up shit creek without a paddle if I didn't immediately agree to write a piece for their programme on that year's Guest of Honour, Gene Wolfe, guy. I said, Have them write me with some details. Soon enough, I was communicated with again. Give us 3000 words (they communicated). Yesterday (they added). For free (they made clear). *Good* words, guy. Because Gene Wolfe had become something of a Magic Lozenge for me, I agreed to do the piece. And did so, very quickly. And sent it off, with a covering letter asking for two copies of the Programme Booklet to be sent me, so that I could see what I'd written, having of course no plans or wherewithal to go to Australia that year, even if I'd much wanted to. I heard nothing. I assumed that no news was good news, and that the piece fit requirements. Months passed. Judith Hanna and Joseph Nicholas, London friends who had attended Aussiecon Two, returned from Hyperborea. Thought you'd like to see your piece, said Judith, and very kindly gave me a copy of the Programme Booklet, where indeed the Gene Wolfe piece (in corrected form it appears below) reposed, neatly enough, *reasonably* free of literals and the like. From the Aussiecon Two Committee, however, nary a whimper. And certainly no copy of the 3000 word essay I gave them after quite a bit of urgency hype. Funny people. I don't much want to ever meet them. The Australians I dealt with had names, but I'm doing them the favour of not plunging into my files just now *1986*.]

It is October 1983. You are about to meet Gene Wolfe for the first time. He is in London with his wife Rosemary at the behest of the paperback publishers of *The Book of the New Sun*. You drive a borrowed crepitating Volvo through the polished autumn of the West End and park outside the squat, block-long hotel into which they've been booked. This hotel has the appearance of a building far more complex inside than out; there could easily be a garden on the roof, packed with humid sod; and inside there might be flowering plants of an unusual complexity, several mirrored alcoves, a sense of dusk at midday. You are early. The lobby boasts flowering plants, alcoves with mirrors. You sit in an anteroom. Corridors launch twistedly into what might be a vast interior. It is almost time to meet Severian.

You are soon directed further inwards, down one of the corridors, past an utterly silent woman in a uniform and two kraters. You turn into a small chamber where Gene Wolfe sits. He is just completing an interview on tape with Colin Greenland [a London critic and novelist who later took over with Lisa Tuttle the sf class we'll be referring to soon enough *1986*], which will be published in some magazine. Wolfe stands to shake hands. He is in his early fifties, of at least medium height, stocky, bald, calm, competent, simultaneously bonhomous and reserved, candid and crafty; the small-town mayor with a touch of the magus. Or — it was an egregious thought, and one immediately suppressed — Sergeant Bilko as Aslan.

But not Severian, or the iced-over Dennis Alden Weer of *Peace*, or the unnamed narrator of the first part of *The Fifth Head of Cerberus*, whose name, it is possible to work out, is in fact Gene Wolfe. Tracing some lockjaw connection between the physical appearance and behaviour of an author, and the works he has given us out of that body, is, of course, both vulgar and inutile; and most of us have always known, at some level, that corpus and corpse are dissimilar moults. Most of us, all the same, never stop trying to make the connection. We know that the work is entailed by the man; we can never stop hoping for the reverse as well, as though a man were the clothes of what has been said (like Severian). It is hard to stop angling for the world to make as much sense as fiction, as though the Student who dreamt Severian could dream us.

With some authors, at dusk with the light behind them, the trick almost seems to work. At times, even in private, writers like Harlan Ellison or Michael Moorcock or Thomas M Disch or Jerry Pournelle may seem to impersonate (or embody) the worlds of their fiction. Sometimes, for the reader, it is a soothing circumstance that there seems to exist some coterminousness of words spoken and words written that is not merely cosmetic, though in fact this circumstance is precisely cosmetic, a masque. All the same, a starting-place for the interpretation of the works sometimes seems — perhaps not altogether foolishly — to be established. It may be no coincidence that in the case of Gene Wolfe, a man whose fiction offers more problems of interpretation than that of any other author in the field, there is no palpable connection whatsoever. In his introduction to *Plan[e]t Engineering*, Wolfe's most recent collection, David Hartwell makes the same point, though cagily he does not take responsibility for it. He only records, by hearsay, "a complex and silly game played one night among the attendees of the famed Milford SF Writing Conference" in the early seventies; the game was to decide "the writer whose everyday personality seem[ed] to relate least to his written work." Wolfe won.

In any case, in October 1983, the man stands and shakes hands. He is an extremely pleasant, very adult person. The Volvo has a traffic ticket. By a circumbendibus we all arrive, after a passage of time, at the City Literary Institute off Drury Lane, where I've been teaching a University of London class in science fiction for some years. We've been reading *The Book of the New Sun*, whose availability in England Wolfe is in the country to promote. We have been studying the four volumes of his magnum opus for a couple of weeks now. Again and again we've found ourselves snarled up in matters of interpretation — or better, decipherment. Decipherment is the word, because we've hardly begun actually to *interpret* the book. But maybe we've got it all back to front. Maybe we've been seeing puzzles where puzzles, if they do in fact exist, do not really matter. Perhaps, against all our sense of things, *The Book* is actually written in clear. Perhaps — to take an instance — we've been dizzying ourselves unnecessarily over the titles of the four books Severian borrows from the unmistakeably Borgesian library at the heart of the Citadel, the Library whose labyrinthine underground corridors extend — it may be — to the House Absolute itself.

Does the Library, which the world contains, contain the world? And if it *does* contain the world, is this an encompassing to be understood in a figurative sense only, as a kind of literary joke or assonance? Or must the paradox be understood metaphysically, which in Wolfe's world more or less means literally? Severian is borrowing the four books to give them to Thecla, the high-born ("exultant") prisoner in the Matachin Tower, where he is an apprentice torturer. As at least one member of the class is convinced that Thecla is Severian's mother — and most of us are convinced that whoever Severian's mother is, to identify her successfully will represent an essential decipherment of the text — we are most earnestly concerned to work out just what books he is taking to her. But the text is unnervingly and suavely coy. Only one book is named, *The Book of the Wonders of Urth and Sky*. The largest of those remaining seems to be a family history, seemingly of Thecla's own prominent family. The smallest book of all may be a book of prayers, some or all of them perhaps suitable for addressing the Conciliator, whom we know (or think we know) to be an avatar of the Severian of *The Book*, the Severian whose destiny as the New Sun seems determined from the very first paragraph of *The Shadow of the Torturer*, when, after his symbolic birth through near-drowning, he begins to have premonitions about his future. But the fourth and last book, which is never referred to directly, could it, asks a member of the class, be *The Book of the New Sun* itself?

"Ha," says Gene Wolfe, grinning at the members of the class like Sergeant Bilko sitting on a full house, "you're not going to catch me that way."

This may be a hint, but it does not take us in the sf class much beyond the vertigo of decipherment that has been griping at us. Some of us are of the opinion that, because of the nature of the Library, Severian must be in possession of the version of *The Book of the New Sun* that he claims only to conceive of writing when he talks to Master Palaemon at the end of volume four of the tetralogy; it would be this version that we, in this Earth, in 1983, are conceived to have been reading. If this is the case, then the memorious Severian will have had at his finger tips and in his mind's eye, from early youth, a literal transcription of his life from that point on. I'm of the opinion that such a conclusion about the nature of *The Book* would make Severian — who tells his own story as a form of confession and also advocacy — into a narrator so unreliable as to cast every sentence of his story into unending doubt, doubt without egress. In 1983, I prefer to think that if the fourth book is *The Book of the New Sun*, then it must be the version written by the original Conciliator, a shadow of the torturer, where Severian's ascension might be predicted as in parable, but not the details of his course.

Anybody who owns a copy of *Plan[e]t Engineering* may sense or remember something pretty odd at this point. That book was published early in 1984, having been assembled in 1983. It contains an essay, "Books in *The Book of the New Sun*, " in which Gene Wolfe does actually reveal, after his own fashion, the title of that fourth book. It is, of course, *The Book of the New Sun*. But which version? (Ha says Gene Wolfe you're not going to catch me that way.) At one point he says — as I would wish him to — that it is a collection of stories or parables assembled by the Conciliator, the text Dr Talos has at hand when he composes the play which is presented at the House Absolute, with Severian as one of the actors. But Wolfe also refers to the book in terms which — to me — produce a Moebius Strip of metaphysical inturning: "For the library of Master Uhlan is in *The Book of the New Sun*, and *The Book of the New Sun* is in his library. And you are the readers of that book."

So have fun in Australia. Ask Gene a question or two. Expect anything. "Any more questions?" said Gene Wolfe at the end of the session in 1983, genial, eloquent, deeply imperturbable. A member of the class then asked a question about *The Fifth Head of Cerberus*. Certain clues about the narrator's name seemed to lead in one particular direction, he said. Given these clues, could the narrator's name really be Gene Wolfe? Gene glanced at the student in mild surprise. "Why of course," he said, as though he were the last person in the world to have a secret.

The truth, of course, is different. Gene Wolfe may not be the finest writer the science fiction world has yet produced — though I myself do think he almost certainly is — but it is surely the case that he is the science fiction writer least easy to understand at a single reading, as the bemused gaffes of reviewers and critics over the years have so amply demonstrated. After two or three readings, it might seem very dumb to think of *The Book of the New Sun* as a picaresque novel — a novel, that is, in which an agile protagonist or picaro skips his way through a series of unconnected adventures — but take a look at some of the early reviews. [And given the fact that Severian's sword is no more than sharp, that his Claw is the thorn of a rose, that there is no sorcerer in the book not a hierodule in disguise, nor sorcery not explicable in terms of the most orthodox science fiction, it does seem particularly stubborn of critics — see my comment on David Wingrove above — to continue to call the book anything they want to, when all they want to call it is some sort of fantasy *1986*.] It might not seem the brightest possible reading of *Peace* to describe that deeply ironic tale of death and corruption as a nostalgic idyll; but look at the reviews. It might seem superficial to think of *The Fifth Head of Cerberus* as an assemblage of three novellas only remotely interconnected; but it wasn't until the Australian expatriate critic Peter Nicholls wrote an essay on the book for an American compendium that the full plot and thematic integrity of that savage novel began to come clear.

Perhaps what's necessary with Wolfe's work is to train ourselves in the kind of close critical reading of text that serious critics of the Modernist and Post-Modernist novel assume to be absolutely mandatory just for starters, with understanding to come later, after some work has been done. In the sf class I taught in London, we also at one point read *The Fifth Head of Cerberus*; it was my second reading of the book. Between the two readings I'd tackled most of the later work. Being slightly more prepared the second time around, I found the joke about the narrator's name readily decipherable. By dint of attempting to read close up to the words, I came to the conclusion that there was simply no reasonable doubt about what had happened to the anthropologist, John V Marsch; even the exact page — page 233 of the American first edition — where VRT assumes the dead human's identity seemed to be marked incontrovertibly. It was the class's first try at Gene Wolfe. Nobody had noticed that unanswerable shift from human to shape-changing alien, because nobody was initially briefed to attempt to read the text as though every word was intended to bear meaning. But after a few minutes of discussion (as I recollect the evening with a pride that might well airbrush the truth) the class came round, as though a door had been opened, to the efficacy of close reading. After that, no cues from me were needed. And a few months later, they gave *The Book of the New Sun* the kind of preliminary reading I'm absolutely sure it both warrants and demands. Unless you are willing to take the book literally, it will never even begin to unfold into what may be its true exultant shape.

It's been noticed several times already in print — and it's surely a reasonable thing to notice — that most of Gene Wolfe's protagonists are children, and that the most significant of them tell their own stories, as "Gene Wolfe" does, and Den Weer, and Severian. To this observation should be added a significant rider. These protagonists generally tell their stories from a vantage point of years — perhaps many years — subsequent to the events that shaped their lives. Even a relatively simple character like Mark in *The Devil in a Forest* — or, if he is not exactly simple, then the third-person narrative that describes certain events of his early life is comparatively straightforward — even Mark is seen at one point as remembering the *rite de passage* into morally complex adulthood from the vantage of thirty years; and notice how like Wolfe's other heroes Mark is, in his lacking any clear parentage, in his cagey mendacity, in his powerful sexual drive, in the cold that burns when touched. As these characters are telling their stories in the technical format of the *confession*, it may not be surprising that none of their narratives are reliable. (Ha says Severian you're not going to catch me that way.) Their stories are not reliable because memory is not exact, certainly when emotions flood the synapses — except of course for Severian, who never forgets, but then Severian is a liar, as he admits with a frequency sufficient for belief; their stories are not reliable because they are life-arguments, advocacies, presentations of self, the summae of deeply wounded souls.

At first glance the novels and stories seem radically different from one another, and amply demonstrate their author's fertility as a teller of tales; but on a closer reading, it may strike one that something like the same story is being told again and again, the same rite of incarceration and release. (Note, by the way, how similarly oriented within their worlds are the symbolic dwellings of Wolfe's three main protagonists to date: "Wolfe" 's house with the garden on top; Weer's tomb; Severian's House Absolute, which is built underground so that the garden on top is just precisely the surface of the world [and Benjamin Free's house in *Free Live Free*, too, which is like a coffin full of imago/maggots bursting into miracles of birth *1986*]. And note, for instance, the parallel structures of storytelling; and the concealed deaths; and the tales within the tales [that tell in concentrated form the larger stories they nest within, so that the deeper inside you venture, the larger (as in John Crowley's *Little, Big*) you find the world to be *1986*]. And note how stories and novels reflect one another, how "The Eyeflash Miracles" is a stab at the story of Severian; how Little Tib in "Eyeflash" is "really" Ozma in the same way that Severian is "really" Thecla. And so on, and so on.) But there's something more than repetition going on here. It might tentatively be described as a pattern of responses to the chance of escaping from prison — the prison of the self, may be, though that formulation begs quite a few questions — a pattern that has, by the way, evolved significantly over the years. The "Gene Wolfe" of *The Fifth Head of Cerberus*, for instance, could easily be thought of as what one might call a closed clone; each cloned repetition of his line, which is himself, narrows the genetic and metaphysical freedom of each new bearer of the name. On the other hand, the Severian of *The Book of the New Sun*, who is the New Sun himself, who is an "earlier" Severian reborn or twice-told or oft-thought, this memorious self-given Severian is what one might call an opened clone. And in Gene Wolfe's latest published novel, *Free Live Free*, which I've only read once and am therefore not going to try to describe [but see below *1986*], there is an augur of Eden in the title, though surely it is of a threatened paradise, and in the vast movement of return in which the novel ends there is a distinctly prelapsarian air, though surely it is threatened .... It would be unwise to scant that air of threat, but there is an air of something opening in the heart of these later books. It is like the abysses of the cruel world; but it can be likened to love, also.

Ha says Gene Wolfe.

1985.

[The review that follows is taken from the end of a column for *The Washington Post Book World*; the previous review in this column was of Robert A Heinlein's *The Cat Who Walks Through Walls*, and ended with some comments on how very partially he applies the libertarianism of his TANSTAAFL slogan to the characters of this weird novel; in effect, only those whom Heinlein disparages get TANSTAAFL shoved down their throats; "for Lazarus Long and the Chosen Few, the lunch is free. It leaves an odd taste." Then followed the Wolfe review *1986*.]

If there is a free lunch at the end of Gene Wolfe's superlative new comedy of metamorphosis and redemption, then it has been earned. In undertaking first to protect and then to find old Ben Free, the four superficially streetwise protagonists of *Free Live Free* (Arbor House, 1985) must struggle through the comic inferno of a subtly transformed world, and must then gain their hearts' desires only to find them wanting. Only at the end of their adventures will an unmasked Ben Free show them that redemption — true happiness — the real world lies within them, and has in a sense done so all along. He will then send them back through time to redeem their earlier selves by living their own lives anew and transfigured, just as Severian does in Wolfe's great *Book of the New Sun*.

From almost the first page of *Free Live Free*, Wolfe makes it clear that his fable can be read as a loose fantasia on the 1939 film version of *The Wizard of Oz*. When the four finally corner Free at the controls of the vast balsa-wood propeller-driven airplane and time machine through which Wizard-like he rules the world below, the connection is both pointed and deeply comical. But *Oz* is by no means the end of it. *Free Live Free* reads as an attempt to recapture the essence of the world of the American film before the War. Not only *Oz* but *The Maltese Falcon*; not only the young Howard Hawks/Hughes but, more importantly, Frank Capra. In its lucid nostalgia, and in its magic-realist populism, *Free Live Free* is very much *Oz* as Frank Capra might have dreamed it.

Even the limited edition of the book, published last year [1984] by Mark V Ziesing at $45, was so clear and compulsive in the telling that it could be read at one long go. Slightly sharpened at points, [supplied with a Chronology that my proof copy did not have *1986*], and shorn of the dithery Chapter 43 of the original version, *Free Live Free* now flows with an unbroken liquid precision from this world to the last one, from dream to a magically-achieved reality. Like an enormously expanded version of the tales-within-tales that punctuate his earlier novels, *Free Live Free* is an exemplary fable. It is humorous, loving, loyal and true. From an author whose sensibility is complex and serenely chilling, it reads like a present from the heart. It is blessed to give.

The Washington Post//24 November 1985

1986.

Given the sly complexities of the text under consideration, given only a few inches of space to unpack that text, and given an audience it would be unsafe to assume had much familiarity with sf or fantasy, I think this *Washington Post* review of *Free Live Free* might be the most efficient piece of copy I've ever managed to put together. It assumes no secrets and tells no lies. It presents a version of a slippery text I'd still hold to. All the same, in this review and in the earlier material I've put together to make up this sequence of responses to Gene Wolfe's high crafty art, there is surely — I can taste it while correcting and transcribing these pieces — a kind of decorous and perhaps not over-courageous effect of wallowing, in the interpretations put on display here. Of course no one wants to look a fool, though in a moment I'm going to demonstrate how easy it is to look a fool about Gene Wolfe, and there is a natural impulse to avoid coming to a hard reading of a Wolfe story in case one has entirely missed the point of it. At the same time, one should really do him the initial courtesy of assuming that he wishes to be understood (though in fact he may have no such wish). Specifically, one should begin (it will be a bare beginning) to try to make some sense of his major work to date, *The Book of the New Sun.*

Making sense of Gene Wolfe, it seems to me, is initially a job of decipherment. Interpretation of the text must follow its decipherment, must subtend some consensus about the raw configurations of the story itself. Most readers of *The Book* will have undertaken for themselves something of this task, will have made a large number of "hard readings" of points in the text. They will have understood how an apparent work of loose fantasy cashes out in fact as the firmest of sf texts — how, for instance, the Matachin Tower, which seems initially to be some sort of donjon, can turn out on being hard-read to be one of a group of long-disused spaceships. This turn — this translation — most readers will have taken as a model for more serious turns in which the seemingly vague or ambivalent or fantastic or merely colouristic focuses into a hard datum, as though one's eyes had been washed: and the world shines forth in its true array. Using this model of *turning*, readers will have been able to understand the true sanctity — as opposed to the jiggery-pokery sword-and-sorcery magic "power" — of the Claw of the Conciliator, which is "merely" the thorn of a rose. And most readers of the tetralogy will have been forced — forced indeed by Gene Wolfe himself, as he makes it clear that there is *some* mystery to be solved — into making some kinds of speculation about the nature of Severian's secret family, though perhaps not everyone will share my conviction that decipherment can have a stop, and the fuller task of interpretation begin, only when some sense of the identity of that family has been established.

Is there a sister in the text? A father? A mother?

We are told that *Severian* is a name usually given to one of a pair of twins. If there is a sister, she will have been raised in the Witches' Keep in the Citadel, and she may well make some sort of appearance. I have myself gotten nowhere in identifying her, or in tracing any significance that might attach to her presence in *The Book*, though if she does appear I suspect it is on the road to Thrax.

In his essay on *The Book* in *Science Fiction: Ten Explorations* (1986), C N Manlove urges the need for a fervency of interpretation, but seems at times to shy from making firm statements about the raw shape of *The Book* or the identity of its cast. His reading of Dorcas is particularly reticent; while recognizing that she is important to the text, he goes no further than to suggest that she *seems* to have been resurrected (Acts *IX*, 39 provides Biblical sanction, by the way, for both her resurrection and her subsequent occupation), and fails to make any comment on her family connection to Severian. Many readers will have found little real difficulty in identifying Severian's father as Ouen, the waiter in the tree restaurant at the end of the first volume who runs away when he recognizes in Dorcas his mother reborn (after 40 years); and their recognition of Dorcas as Severian's paternal grandmother will have sharpened their response to his affair with her, as well as much else in the text. Professor Manlove's failure to establish this profound linkage vitiates his reading of Dorcas, and in general leaves him standing outside a book he correctly identifies as requiring copious exegetical work. And in so far as he fails to make this relatively simple identification available to his own readers, he fails to bring *The Book of the New Sun* into focus.

Dorcas and Ouen (we will see that his name is also significant) are fairly straightforward figures to place, and the reader will have been richly rewarded for doing the work of placing them. It is by no means as simple a task to identify Severian's mother, or even to be more than intuitively certain she inhabits the text, subcutaneously informing Severian's grasp of the world. There is nothing apodictic about the signs of her presence, and I for one feel a kind of vertigo — as though my interpretive faculties had become unglued at the task, had overheated, become feverish — at the thought of trying to pin her down. Nor am I by any means certain of the richness of the reward for making a fix that seems inherently contestable — for the miracle of most of Wolfe's conundrums is that, once solved, they seem perfectly obvious, and enrich one's reading. All the same, the text does seem to ask one to look for a mother, though ultimately it may make mock of one's efforts. At the time of writing the review of *The Citadel of the Autarch* reprinted above, I did in fact arrive at a tentative identification of Severian's mother, one which seemed to fit the basic criterion of enriching my reading of the text, but one about which I could feel no security, nor do I now. If I therefore present some speculations about her, it is less because I expect I am correct than it is to demonstrate the kind of deciphering tactics *The Book of the New Sun* seems to demand of readers who become engaged in its conundrums.

Every woman in *The Book of the New Sun*, except Dorcas, is of course a candidate. *In some fashion* she will need to have been in a position to have slept with Ouen about 20 years previously; she will have called herself Catherine; she will have had some relationship to an order of monials, but not necessarily that of postulant; and because of some trouble she is in she will have been picked up by the law when pregnant and given birth to Severian while inside the Matachin Tower. Beyond those criteria, she could be anyone. Some candidates, perhaps wrongly, got short shrift. I spent no time on Agia, for instance, nor on the head of the Pelerine order of monials, nor on Thecla's sister, nor on Jolenta, nor on the mother of the boy-Severian on the road from Thrax. Tom Disch — one of several friends and colleagues to whom I mentioned the problem and my sense of its significance — passed swiftly over some plausible names and settled on Morwena, the woman Severian executes at the beginning of *The Claw of the Conciliator*, on the basis that her name sort of rhymed with Ouen's, but he was joking. After this, only four obvious candidates remained.

Cyriaca seemed plausible enough, up there in windowless Thrax. She was about the right age, she had been involved with monials in her youth and had escaped them, she had been travelling at the right time, and she even makes a motherly reference to Severian. But I did not like the choice, nor do I now. It was, and is, a *boring* choice, nor would making it much help to explain Severian's seemingly elaborate masking of his mother's identity — an objection which does not apply to my final choice; Cyriaca was simply too lightweight to bear the burden of the secrecy that surrounds the mystery. (In a personal letter, Gene Wolfe also — *I think* — rejected her, while at the same time he refused to make any positive statement on the issue.)

Thecla seemed much more likely, and Greg Benford has said he'd assumed she was Severian's mother long ago, on reading *The Shadow of the Torturer* when it first came out. The blood seeping under the door of her cell (he thought) was an analogue of birth blood; and something about her behaviour and appearance also triggered him. Thecla is of course ostensibly much too young, but we *are* told that exultants — in a fashion connected to the clone/khaibits who impersonate them — enjoy extended lifespans, so that she might be much older than she looks. She is very tall. Her reaction on first seeing Severian *may* relate as much to seeing her son (who, we are told, bears an extraordinary resemblance to his father) as to seeing her torturer. But he *is* nearly identical to Ouen, and her reaction, all considered, does seem to fall short of what one might expect (as does Cyriaca's when she first sees him under similarly heightened circumstances). There is no hint that she is in fact older than she seems, nor that she has ever called herself Catherine, nor that she has ever had any connection with an order of monials, nor that she has ever been imprisoned before. And, most significantly, her central role in the text as a sort of co-protagonist and deep sister is neatly exemplified — and exhausted — by Severian's ingestion of her.

Valeria too would seem simply too young — and too unsurprised — though the language Gene Wolfe uses to describe her and the Atrium of Time which fronts her residence, plus the undeveloped but intensely felt significance of the fact that Severian goes to her at the close of the tetralogy, all does lead to some sense of hushed heightened *burden*. There is something pregnantly odd about Valeria ("I am all the sisters we breed. And all the sons.") and the Atrium of Time which, remember, is not named after the sundials that cluster within it: they have been placed there because it is the Atrium of Time. We also remember that in volume one Severian arrives for the first time at the Atrium from underground — is reborn into it — after having followed the dog Triskele's three-legged paw-marks into the mazes under the Citadel. Seeing the light of the sun, he climbs up into the Atrium, a high narrow courtyard into which indeed the sun — the sun is always significant in this text — is shining. It is as though the sun is always shining into the Atrium: as though Time were held in its palm. Severian then meets Valeria, who bears the name of a Roman family famous for having served Emperors over the span of a millenium, and is deeply struck by her. A thousand pages later, when as Autarch he wants to find her again, he cannot, with all the devices at his command, locate the Atrium of

Time at all. Only when he once again traces Triskele's path, only by following the *exact route* he had once followed, the marks of Triskele's paws and his own feet still visible in the deep passages of the Citadel, can he come once again into the sunlit Atrium. This experience exactly replicates an experience earlier in the same volume, when Severian can only reach the house of Master Ash, who is a traveler in the Corridors of Time, by following the precise route laid down for him. Once within the holy confines of the rose-choked Atrium of Time, Severian then speaks Autarchal words of power, which Valeria's habitation clamorously recognizes, and the novel ends. All in all, Valeria sounds more like a wife-to-be than a mother.

So we have a shallow aunt, a deep sister, and a wife-to-be. We do not yet have a mother. We come to the woman who serves in the ceremony at the Matachin Tower in which Severian becomes a journeyman torturer. As far as Severian claims to know, this woman appears only once a year, when it comes time to perform the ceremony of induction, and has been doing so as long as he — who forgets nothing — can remember. In the ceremony, she takes on the role of Saint Katherine, patroness of the order of torturers; before she can be strapped to the Wheel to be tortured (as was the original Saint Catherine of Alexandria), the Wheel breaks forth in roses; after she is bound to it, it dissolves. Her age is not easy to fix; as far as Severian can judge, she has never changed (one thinks of the masked hierodules). She is intimate with the Matachin Tower, and may once have been an inmate there. She will certainly have seen Severian frequently enough, over the years of his childhood and adolescence, not to be surprised at his startling resemblance to a possible former lover. Severian's reaction to her is extraordinary, and is couched by Gene Wolfe with that deceiving air of intense lucidity he shifts into only at moments of high significance, when through layers of crystalline syntax the reader can fall for ever. She is tall, slender, "dark of complexion, dark of eye, raven of hair. Hers was such a face as I have never seen elsewhere, like a pool of pure water found in the midst of a wood." Severian then performs the ceremony, cutting off her head, which indeed is only wax, made in her semblance. Something inchoate here reaches for expression. This Katharine/Catherine represents a pattern of associations of a very strong order, and I for one am disinclined to challenge it. But if we are to grant that this woman is Severian's mother, who then is this woman?

We come to one of the most difficult passages in *The Book* (p. 109-110 of *The Shadow of the Torturer*). We enter the Borgesian house of mirrors of the Corridors of Time, where semblance meets semblance, significances multiply. After the ceremony, having drunk too much, Severian is taken to his bunk, where he has what seems to be a dream like others he has recounted. Only later are we are told that these "dreams" are not dreams at all but genuine experiences in the Corridors. In his "dream," a semblance of Catherine is succeeded by a whiff of Thecla's perfume as used by her khaibit in the House Azure, which is itself a house of mirrors; Severian then becomes the risen Christ. We must now enter dangerous territory; Catherine may be no one but herself, her absences from the Matachin Tower explainable by her presence in the Corridors of Time. Perhaps later — in the fifth volume perhaps — Severian will meet her again, and she will be as she has ever been, with her haunting eyes, her face (her mask) like a shadowed pool; and they will speak together. But this seems — almost literally — an escapist reading of the text; *The Book* in our hands (it seems to me) needs to *contain* Catherine. Let us return to the khaibit, who is not seen but smelled: only Catherine is seen. Any reference to the khaibit evokes her doyen, as does any reference to the House Azure. The reader will remember that when he first meets this figure, earlier in the same first volume of *The Book*, Severian is greatly affected by the encounter. The doyen speaks with the voice of a contralto, his eyes seem like windows through which it is possible to see "a sky of summer drought." On remembering that the sky of Urth is dark even at midday, the reader will udnerstand that Severian's image is one of translucent darkness, "like a pool of pure water found in the midst of a wood," it may be. In any case, Severian's response to the doyen strikingly resembles his response to Catherine. They are intrinsicate. As we discover only in Volume Two, however, the doyen of the House Azure, who first introduces Severian to the khaibit Thecla, and who is now evoked in the person of his mother, is in fact the Autarch. As though a semblance has been discarded, we never see the "young woman" of the ceremony again.

But how can we be persuaded that an unfantastical reading of *The Book of the New Sun* could lead to the conclusion that Severian's mother is the Autarch? Is the maid not sufficient in herself? Perhaps we can put the question of sex to one side for a moment, and ask if it is at all plausible to think that the Autarch can *play* the role of Catherine? If it is simply a question of disguises, we know the answer to be in the affirmative. When we first meet "him," the Autarch is, after all, playing a role in the House Azure, which itself parodies the House Absolute, and throughout the tetralogy there are hints that "he" may well haunt the text in a variety of semblances, gathering information, haunting the Corridors of Time. We do know, not at all incidentally, that "he" has long had a privy source of information in the Matachin Tower itself. Much later, of course, in *The Citadel of the Autarch*, we find out that the Autarch is in fact *legion*, having ingested the memories of all previous Autarchs (including the first Severian's) as part of the assumption of Autarchy that Severian himself undergoes. It is intrinsicate with the condition of Autarchy (remember that Severian, having at first ingested only Thecla, is more than once mistaken for her) that the Autarch wear many faces.

The text does offer a series of widely separated cues. The Autarch, as we know, is an androgyne, having been de-sexed by the hierodules for failing to bring in the New Sun. There is, of course, no reason to insist that this mysterious de-sexing process could not transform a woman as well as a man. Throughout the text, whenever Severian sees the Autarch's profile on a coin of the realm, he first assumes that the profile is female. Early in the first volume, it is recorded that the apprentices in the Matachin Tower have speculated that the Autarch may be a woman dressed as a man; it can be assumed that they know of the consequences of failing to bring in the New Sun, and that their speculations must be rooted in something more than the mere fact of androgyny. With regard to the de-sexing, it is of course understood that it took place some time after the Autarch ascended the throne; by definition some time after the birth of Severian. (A further exploration, only profitably to be entered upon on the surety that the current speculation fits the text, might seek to fix the date of the Autarch's ascent, whether before or after Severian's conception: if the former, then Severian would be, of course, in a sense, his own mother.) In any case, in the intimate dialogue that precedes the Autarch's death in volume four, he/she records to Severian having been involved about twenty years previously in vaguely criminal activities — just as Ouen had been, and at about the same time: which gives opportunity. It is possible to deduce from utterances the Autarch has made that at the same time he/she was taken off by the authorities. In conversation, Gregory Feeley has noted the unusual way in which Gene Wolfe has couched the Autarch's utterances at this point. When the Autarch says to Severian of his/her activities at that time, ". . .that would be in about the year you were born, I suppose . . ." for the only time in the tetralogy a phrase is marked off by ellipses. In a writer of the acute consciousness of style Gene Wolfe everywhere displays, this pair of ellipses is a marker of considerable signifiance;

it is, once again, a syntax through which the reader can fall for ever. It might be mentioned at this point that the Autarch more than once addresses Severian (and no one else) as "My son." This may be a standard form of Autarchal address, but if that were the case one might expect Severian to use the same locution when he becomes Autarch himself; and he does not.

Finally there is the name Ouen. We know that throughout the tetralogy names, from Dorcas to Triskele, have offered significant analogies from our own world. The Ouen who most appositely supplies a sense of fitting analogy is that Owen Tudor (d 1461) who comes from Wales to the English court and sleeps with a woman named Catherine. *She is the queen-mother.* As Henry VII, their grandson ascends the throne and brings to an end the Wars of the Roses. England enters a new age, which will culminate in the reign of Elizabeth, who is often figured as Astraea. Hermetic images of the rule of a new sun constantly infiltrate the language of those who would do honor to the Tudors, whose badge—like Severian's—is a Rose.

So.

There remains the problem of Severian's concealing the nature of his secret family. This may be explained in part—for he is, after all, only a creature of fiction—as simply reflecting Gene Wolfe's almost invariable refusal to make clear expository statements about the deep realities that govern the shape of his best work. All the same, Severian is a clear example of the typical SF protagonist who, by remembering the *truth* about himself and the universe, becomes the saviour of that universe. The entire narrative of *The Book of the New Sun* is ostentatiously the act of what in rhetoric is known as *anamnesis.* ("In anamnesis, the person acknowledges who he is, who his father and mother really are . . . even when such knowledge is horrible as with Oedipus. In anamnesis we 'remember who we are' and the memory is placed in a definite social context; on the contrary, in moments of nostalgia we admit that we are lost." D E Richardson in *The Sewanee Review,* Winter 1981, p. 136.) Like Oedipus at the end, Severian knows who he is, which involves knowing who his parents are; but, unlike Oedipus, he is a liar, if only by omission. The reason for this may be—I'm half-convinced that it must be—related to the function of the text he gives us. Although it is couched as a confession, *The Book of the New Sun* is in fact a political document (whose full import will presumably unfold in the sequel Gene Wolfe is now reportedly completing); it is a position paper for redemption. Under these circumstances, it is perhaps unsurprising that Severian, self-declared advocate of Vodalus's opposition to the very concept of Autarchy, should seek to obscure his blasphemous and bastard connection to the very heart of a world whose Autarchs (it will be remembered) are forbidden to found dynasties.

As far as a case can be made (by me) out of this interminable vertigo of hints for decipherment, a case for deriving conclusions from a particular style of reading Gene Wolfe has been made. There is one further point to suggest about the Autarch, however, one which may seem frivolous, but which all the same goes to the heart of how I conceive Gene Wolfe to work. Readers may have noted that, of all characters of any importance in *The Book of the New Sun*, the Autarch is the only one who goes unnamed. Previous Autarchs not only have names but are (I think always) given soubriquets as well. Even Severian, as Autarch, is known as Severian the Lame. So what then is the Autarch's name? If there is a secret name embedded in the text, can it be anything but Catherine? But does she have a nickname as well, if only as a releasing device in Gene Wolfe's mind? At this point a digression is called for. In that 1983 sf class I mentioned in the Worldcon piece printed above, Gene Wolfe talked for a while about the first of the tales within the text of *The Book*, "The Tale of the Student and His Son." Central to his shaping of the tale (he told us) were two plays on words, one fairly obvious, the other — the more important one — both obscure and maybe frivolous-seeming. The easier wordplay involved the ironclad "ship"/monster that the Son — the man fleshed from dreams — finds at the heart of the watery labyrinth into which he has sailed; this monster is called the Monitor, after the ironclad warship from the American Civil War, but as the man shaped from dreams is clearly a version of Theseus, then the monster is clearly a version of the Minotaur. Many readers will have registered this pun; fewer, I suspect, will have registered the more important (though indeed only subtextual) one, the one that offers so clear an illustration of the workings of Gene Wolfe's mind. For the Student in the city of pale towers, fleshing *Theseus* out of dreams is just the same as writing a *thesis* out of the primordial Word. In the beginning (in the Library of the Autarch) is the Word. Theseus (or Severian, for the story is clearly a parable) is the Word (or The Book of the New Sun) made flesh. *Theseus/thesis*: that is how, in the procreative secrecy of his art, Gene Wolfe works. We return to the Autarch, to the Minotaur. I spoke to Greg Feeley on the telephone about some of these conundrums. I mentioned to him the fact that the Autarch had no name.

— Right (he said), and no soubriquet either, unlike the other Autarchs. I wonder (he added) what the Autarch's name actually is?

— Catherine the Wheel (I said).

— But how do you spell Wheel? (he said).

— W-e-a-l (I said).

A weal is a welt, of course, and could stand for the scar inflicted on Catherine by the hierodules when they desexed her. But far more importantly, weal (I take *Webster's New World Dictionary* as likely to give a commonly accepted definition) is a substantive meaning "a sound or prosperous state; well-being, welfare; *the body politic.* " (My italics.) So. The Autarch, who is legion, who is the body politic of the state, who is the mother of the New Sun, is Catherine the Weal.

//Florida 1986//

INDEX

(Boldface indicates review of an author or work.)

www.ingramcontent.com/pod-product-compliance
Lightning Source LLC
Chambersburg PA
CBHW030814310726
48980CB00006B/499/J

* 9 7 8 1 5 8 7 1 5 3 8 4 6 *